The Ascension of Heidi

A Longhaired Dachshund

Honoring Animals as Spiritual Beings

At 16 years old, Heidi ascended her body
to the Realms of Infinite Grace
leaving only footprints in the snow.

This is the profound and poignant
understanding of how she accomplished it.

A Reverence for Life Presentation

All rights cosmically reserved!
Copyright 2024
Second edition

This book is an update and expansion of
The Ascension of Heidi on Kindle (2016).
After the author's Ascension (!)
This book goes public domain.

Except for the use of brief quotations
in enthusiastic reviews
please contact the author for permission
to use or quote any of the following material.

June Sananjaleen Hughes
sananda444@gmail.com
www.gardenofsananda.com
Sananda, Rectortown, Virginia

Photos by the author:
front cover, Tiggy and Heidi
back cover, Loreli and Buddha
in the Garden of Sananda.

Design and layout, Mary Carnahan
Triangle cover detail, Freepik

In Honor of Heidi

This book is very thought provoking. It makes you realize that all animals come with a specific purpose, and unlike us they seem to know that purpose. ~ *Linda Gareh-Applegate*

I am so inspired by Heidi! It is really packed with parallel dimension information that I feel relates to all the kingdoms. I have a whole new understanding of our Ascension! ~ *Rev Miriam Absurd, ImaginalLiving.org*

Heidi brings new insight into what we think is reality. ~ *Lorraine Nurko*

This book is a love story which stirred me deeply, compellingly told in beautiful prose, with so much love and light pouring through. The author is gifted at bridging the worlds of animals and humans, making the communications barriers dissolve and disappear. Heidi's story is suggestive of far greater capacities within the animal kingdom than we might ever have imagined. ~ *Nancy Seifer, ATreeOfLight.org*

I love the story of Heidi so much! A delightful read for anyone wanting to experience a true story about ascension and for anyone who has ever loved a dog. ~ *Terra Thomas, HummingBirdFarm.org*

These words are such a high vibration. Supremely personal love that is divine. Receiving the perfection in which it is given. A note that these communions are sung too ~ they carry this chord, the song that they sing is the same, no matter how different the stories, it is the same melody. You can hear that music. ~ *Gita Nash*

Heidi's story means a lot to me. I have read and re-read it several times. The account is so detailed and so well-articulated that I could not stop reading. Later I recited the story to my kids. They will not sleep until I tell them about Heidi. Each day I repeat the same story, yet they are not bored. They have made a wonderful connection and spiritual bond with Heidi. I know each time I say her name, Heidi is present in my home in spirit. ~ *Padmini Nidumolu, LeanInAgile.org*

I loved the Heidi story. So much there I didn't know, and is giving me a lot to think about. Lots I can convey to my cat Mei Ling, although I am beginning to see that she probably knows a lot of them already! ~ *Rennee Loustaunau*

The highlight of this book is learning about the amazing spirituality of animals, and what precious missions of love they have agreed to perform. It is rich with insights into the incredible implications of our own spiritual and multidimensional nature. And I love the idea that we all can bring from our own hearts a Love Flame as Gretel did. I am asking Gretel and the others to show me how. I'm incredibly grateful to be introduced to these master teachers in little dog form. ~ *Janice Coyle, NewEarthVisioningProject.com*

I loved reading Heidi! The messages are simply Divine! I look forward to sharing with many in South Africa! ~ *Anthea Torr, IAmFree.co.za*

What an extraordinary encounter. Heidi was obviously a master and demonstrated a potential that is expressed by the highest masters in some of the more esoteric spiritual lineages such as Dzogchen in Tibetan Buddhism. For an animal (other than human) to demonstrate this capacity is extremely rare if not unheard of. ~ *Tom and Judi Kenyon, TomKenyon.com*

Foreword

As an avid reader of hundreds of spiritual and nature related books, I can't think of any other book that tells so much about the spiritual nature of animals. It offers so much and will expand the minds of so many. There is information, adventure, wisdom, and a uniquely charming writing style. The descriptions of ascension are the best I have ever read, simple and eloquent words that speak to the highest.

The dogs' descriptions of their journeys to other dimensions are fun and inspirational. They teach about the joy of adventure, with no limit to the experiences available in consciousness ~ testament to the spirituality of all animals. They have souls, they are multidimensional, they have specific missions, they roam the galaxy ~ the universe, as light beings, or fairies, or whatever is required. They taught me so much about our own infinite potential to explore.

Something about their fun, their wisdom, and the beautiful poetic writing of their scribe, June Sananjaleen Hughes, drew me intimately into their journeys, bringing a clarity and vividness to the many profound spiritual truths taught by these angels of the animal kingdom. Very liberating to the soul to engage in these extraordinary stories.

After reading The Ascension of Heidi, my spiritual insights and understanding expanded to the point of being floored ~ uplifted by the amazing presence of each dog or animal on these pages. Plus the discovery that their consciousness is more expanded than ours!

This wonderful book has expanded everything within me, and brought so much wisdom, joy, inspiration, and love. In amazement, I wonder ~ how can a book about the spirituality of dogs do so much to help and heal? How can such little characters have such an enormous impact? Because this is their mission. The one I cherish most being how much more my heart has been opened.

Janice Coyle
NewEarthVisioningProject.com

Introduction

*Dedicated to a Higher Order of Truth
and Remembrance of Being.
And to the expansion in human consciousness
that animals do so much to quicken.
To all who Serve in Canine Form,
and all the countless Others ~ loved and unloved.*

*In Love they came ~ in silence taught,
captured my heart ~ and left in Grace*

The purpose of this book is to promote awareness of the spiritual nature of animals, and to encourage understanding of their own divine purpose. It is now thirty years since the Ascension of Heidi, but the truths she told, the concepts revealed, are timeless. This expanded version of her original little booklet includes the ascension stories of the other nine little longhaired dachshunds, plus many Ascension-related quotes and memoirs of other animals. Heidi and her mother Gretel were standard size dachshunds, the others were all miniatures, meaning they weighed between seven and ten pounds.

Many of the quotes are taken from Ascended and Free, a Forcefield of Divine Consciousness that provides a Sacred Template for individual and group Lightwork. Presented by a group of dedicated Light Beings and offering information that comes from the Spiritual Hierarchy ~ Ascended Masters and Great Cosmic Beings. Information which I originally received through a small monthly journal called Group Avatar, and now known as Ascended and Free.

Regarding the name 'Sananda'! We, Heidi, Gretel and I, came to the small village of Rectortown in 1985. For two years I searched for a name for our Space of Love, and then I read the word Sananda! The book described this Being as the Cosmic Christ and I didn't know what to make of that, but pretty soon my car tags, my email, and a sign at the bottom of the garden all said ~ SANANDA! My current understanding allows that Sananda is a Great Being or Forcefield of Cosmic Light and Goodness.

For those unfamiliar with the Violet Fire, it is a Cosmic Forcefield of Sacred Flame, a very powerful energy with the ability to purify and transmute lower vibrational energies. This Violet Fire, or Flame, an Agent of Transformation, can be invoked and directed towards any person, place, condition or situation in need of purification, protection, compassion and/or Freedom. It is specifically associated with the Ascended Master Saint Germain and the Law of Forgiveness. The Violet Fire Angels are individual forcefields of energy that may be called upon for a blessing at any time.

Portals and vortices are also mentioned quite frequently. A very brief definition is that a portal is usually thought of as an opening or doorway, which can be temporary or long term. It can also be dormant. A vortex is somewhat like a whirlpool of energy from the earth's core that has risen to the surface, and may create a portal, or doorway to other realms or dimensions.

The entire Garden of Sananda is considered a vortex in that it pulsates at a higher frequency or vibration than the surrounding territory. Described by almost all who come as 'magical'. A place of peace and serenity. The house and garden are filled with crystals and windchimes. Flowers seem ever in bloom, and over the years there have been many spiritual workshops, playdays, and presentations by people from all over the world. Each of which has helped raise the vibration of the land and all thereon.

Many things have led me to the understanding that Masters and Teachers of the Higher Realms can manifest in any way or form they choose. An animal may not always be what most of us think of as an animal. They come to us as teachers, healers, friends and companions. They may even be emanations of our own angelic selves. The intent of this book is to foster awareness of the evolutionary role of animals in the expansion of human consciousness. I dedicate it to those who comprise the animal kingdoms as we know them ~ and because it makes a difference in the lives of those who read it.

Acknowledgements and websites are given at the end of this book.

From the Same Author

Whale Wisdom Dolphin Joy
Paperback and Kindle

The Dolphin Ones
Paperback and Kindle

Joanna's World
a children's book
Paperback

The Sananda Ascension Essences
flower and mineral infusions from the Garden of Sananda
(manual in process of update)

Coming Attractions

Remembering Their Joy
Profound insights from animals
who have made or are about to make their transition.
Plus suggestions on how to 'animal communicate' yourself.

Paneurhythmy
a Celebration with Nature
a Path to Ascension

~ ~ ~ ~ ~

June Sananjaleen Hughes

sananda444@gmail.com
www.gardenofsananda.com

Epigraph

In our Ascended and Free Declaration, we state:
'In Union with the Royal Kingdoms of Angels and Elementals.'
Your relationship with Heidi embodies this Truth,
and in so embodying it,
brings us all closer to our own Ascension.
In her Ascended State Heidi continues to bless us all.
May the Light of God ever expand!

~ *Love, Ascended and Free*

Table of Contents

In Honor of Heidi

Foreword

Introduction

From the Same Author

Epigraph

Table of Contents

Part One   The Ascension of Heidi   1

January 22, 1994 ~ Heidi's Joy	2
January 24, 1994 ~ Her Body Will Not Be Found	6
January 25, 1994 ~ The Beam of Light	7
January 28, 1994 ~ The Rose	8
February 2, 1994 ~ Logic vs. Frequency	9
February 4, 1994 ~ The Great Rays	11
February 7, 1994 ~ Fusion	13
February 9, 1994 ~ The Song of Freedom	14
March 2, 1994 ~ Angel That She Is	16
March 4, 1994 ~ The Ascension Vortex	17
March 6, 1994 ~ Definition of Ascension	18
March 7, 1994 ~ Blanket of Light	19
March 8, 1994 ~ Fountain of Youth	21
March 10, 1994 ~ The Furry Fairy	22
March 10, 1994 ~ The Cloud of Peace	22
March 16, 1994 ~ The State of I AMNESS	23
May 1, 1994 ~ Was and Is!	25
May 5, 1994 ~ Others Did It Too	25
May 6, 1994 ~ Angels	29
June 5, 1994 ~ The Bondage of Love	29
January 1995 ~ The Game of Life	30
January 1995 ~ The Merkabah	36

January 1995 ~ The Dimensional Doorway	40
January 1995 ~ The Call to Ascension	41
New Moon January 1995 ~ Heidi's Love	42
She Walked Away	43
The End	44

The Ascension of Gretel   45

The Ascension of Tiggy   60

The Ascension of Loreli   72

The Ascension of Lorna and Lilly   87

The Ascension of Candace   97

The Ascension of Olivia   108

The Ascension of Primrose   111

The Ascension of Schatzi   121

The Flame 1995   129

The Ascension of Others   135

The Ascension of Emma 2019   135

The Ascension of Digit 1995   136

The Ascension of Tiny Mike 1987   136

The Ascension of Amanda 1995   138

The Ascension of Natty 1984   139

Part Two   Ascension Related Concepts   141

The Concept of Ascension in Relation to Gravity	147
Ascension Related Concepts	151
The Dolphin Call to Ascension	156

Part Three   Animals as Spiritual Beings — 157

The Purpose of Animals in Our Lives — 157
The Council of Animals Speak — 160
Animals as Teachers and Healers — 166
Communicating with Animals — 172
Transition — 176

Blessed Is the Heart — 181

Acknowledgements — 182

Sananda Ascension Essences — 184

Paneurhythmy — 192

About the Author — 198

Part One
The Ascension of Heidi

a longhaired Dachshund

This is the Sound of one dog's Ascension.
Her personal and permanent return to Light,
and the Love she never lost.
The Love she never stopped giving and sharing and Being.

It was winter and the land was a frozen waste of solid ice like none had ever known. Cattle and horses in the surrounding fields were in much distress, for they could not stand, they could not keep their feet beneath them. The very birds were frozen in their trees.

Yet Heidi's heart was filled with joy.
A joy she could not veil.
A joy that shone from her eyes.
Expressed in laughter and gladness
as Heidi danced the Heidi dance
bouncing gently, jubilant with song
her eyes on mine.
A dance created for Shumala,
her special friend, and mine.
And Heidi rejoiced in sliding on the ice,
tromping through half frozen mud,
rummaging through frozen birdseed.
And Heidi knew a freedom in her heart
that brought her joy untold.
For Heidi was going home,
back to the realms from whence she came.
And only Heidi knew, a secret no-one shared,
That this was Heidi's Ascension Day.

January 22, 1994 ~ Heidi's Joy

It was true. All week we have been iced in. Temperatures below zero. And 16 ½ year old Heidi has had a most wonderful time. She has skated down the embankment to the road, tramped up and down the half frozen muddy stream, excavated frozen birdseed, quarried for frozen poop, and munched on frozen birds. She has pursued the concrete loaf of bread, (one of my culinary disasters), that even the birds can't dent.

She has galloped up and down on the ice without going anywhere. Each day I must crawl over the frozen waste and rescue her. She laughs, lying upside down in my arms, her eyes on mine. Reading my soul. Sharing her love. She dances with laughter. Her heart sings with joy. For Heidi is riding the crest of an energy wave that will take her far and high. Today was easier, for we had a light snow, and Heidi pranced and bounced and played in a manner most delightful and quite unusual for her. Out in the snow she did the Heidi-dance, bouncing back and forth from one front foot to the other, ears flapping, eyes shining. What's up Heidi? I said. Unsuspecting. Unaware. Unknowing.

There are no grey hairs on Heidi. She is ageless. Her rich, dark mahogany coat is magnificent. With bright eyes and sense of smell undiminished she can locate and extract cookie crumbs from a visitor's pocket, whether they flung their coat on chair or floor. Admittedly she is a bit absent minded at times; *Are you sure we've had breakfast, mum?* And she is most certainly rather deaf, although Dachshund hearing tends to a selectiveness that varies according to whether the sound in question is food oriented ~ or not.

At 10.30 pm last night, Heidi wanted out. Usually, we are all in bed by this time. My bed. Tiggy and Loreli, the two smaller and younger longhaired Dachshunds, Heidi and me. But last night was different. A fire had made the room snug and warm, and I was reading. The three dogs were piled on top of each other in one of their little cuddler beds, deep asleep beneath their fake fur blanket. Abruptly, the blanket came to life and Heidi bounded out of bed. Normally, by 9 pm she was in such a deep sleep that I had to carry her to bed when I went. Now she was all action, and I supposed she had sensed a passing bunny; *Gotta go out, mum! Gotta go* OUT! Alright, Heidi! Alright! The other two caught her excitement and sped with her through the opened door, into the light fresh snow. It was a beautiful night, but cold, and Tiggy and Loreli came racing back inside very quickly.

Heidi never came back.

The moon was bright and the sky alive with stars, and although I searched past midnight, I could find no sign, no tracks, that Heidi had left the garden. Repeatedly, I was drawn back to an area between the tall pine trees and the well. A large crystal is stationed here, guardian and keeper of records. Every time I passed this crystal I noticed, about three feet from it, and towards the pines, a set of footprints, pawprints, that seemingly didn't go anywhere, they just stopped. That's funny, I thought; *those footprints don't go anywhere.* Well, I'll deal with that in the morning ~ now I must look for Heidi. Even then, even before I had pulled on my boots and coat and gloves and hat I knew, deep inside, that Heidi would not be found. I knew that Heidi had gone.

In the past, not so long ago, this was my worst possible scenario, to have my dog disappear and never be found. But now, I could feel no panic, no anxiety, only acceptance and surrender, and so, unbelievable as it may sound, I went back to bed. But because we are programmed to look for lost things, to be accountable, I set the alarm clock to wake me every hour, so I could run around the house, open each door and look for Heidi. Of course she wasn't there. I knew she wouldn't be there before I opened the door. Next morning I repeated the search but could feel no sorrow. I felt no reason to alert the neighbors or put-up signs for a lost dog. Again, I noted the tracks by the well. And again I thought; I'll deal with that later. Now, I must look for Heidi. The implication was just too great for this present moment.

And Enoch walked with God:
and he was not; for God took him.
~ Genesis 5.24, King James Bible

A few years earlier, many of us had listened over and over and over, to a set of five audio tapes from Erik Klein speaking about Ascension, and

I had started telling people, three people to be precise; *I know that Heidi is going to take her body with her when she goes.* But one can't stay on a high like that forever, and I forgot about Heidi going anywhere. And anyway, I had assumed she would go from her own bed, or mine. I thought I would wake up one morning and find Heidi gone. It never dawned on me that she would vanish into the great outdoors, with no proof. But then of course, the snow was 'proof'. Much later, I was to realize, that she needed to be in a special place, and she needed to be alone. Just as Elijah (Kings 2, Verse 2), was sent to a special place by the Lord, so that he could be taken up in a chariot of Fire.

Friends came for lunch. Friends of Heidi's, friends of mine. Jim stayed outside, scouting the perimeter of the garden, looking for tracks. Eventually he came in, a funny look on his face; "There's a set of footprints out there that don't go anywhere," he said. The exact same words I had thought in my mind the night before. And I experienced a surge of excitement. A growing sense of elation. Jubilation!

After my friends left, I meditated. I told Heidi how much I loved her. I thanked her, that one as great as she had lived with me. Always had I termed her my equal. Always had I called her an angel. Always had I thought of her as pure Spirit. I didn't know why I thought or called her that, I just did. I took the essence of Fluorite to help me in releasing her, and the essence of Peony (flower and mineral essences that I make here in the Garden of Sananda) to assist me in releasing myself, forgiving myself for anything less than perfect that I had or had not done in caring for or seeking for Heidi. A great sigh escaped me, and I understood that I was her guardian and caretaker. And that was the nearest I came to tears, when I remembered how much I loved her. Words flowed into my mind:

Released in love she flew,
released with love she grew.
And her great wings unfurled, stretched
and reached across the midnight sky,
their unfoldment triggered by forgiveness.
And they beat mightily upon the air,
carrying the one they bore to realms of Light,
and Peace and Love, where one as great as she

could blaze and anchor the Flame of Forgiveness
into a higher realm than the one she left.
And from this vantage point
was she connected to that one on Earth
in whom she placed her trust, to whom she gave her love.
For she was not familiar with the human life,
the human frequency,
and found it hard at times to honor their path.
And now her work complete,
the anchorage of the Flame she bore
is buried in the land she walked.
And others may take up this Flame
and hold it true in Heidi's name. God bless.
We are the Brotherhood of Light,
and Heidi is the Lighted One
We welcome home this glorious day.

I did not understand the reference to Heidi and forgiveness. I thought perhaps it must be connected to the words I spoke as I took the Peony. I was aware that two days earlier we, the planet and all life thereon, had moved under the influence of the Seventh Ray, the Solar Aspect of Deity depicting Compassion, Transmutation, and Freedom. And that the Electronic Pattern of the month allowed all life seeking Freedom to reintegrate into the Whole through the Law of Forgiveness, the Violet Flame. The thought crossed my mind to wonder if Heidi was a Violet Fire Angel. I knew also that the recent seven planetary line up at the time of the new moon had created yet another open door, a stargate or portal, an increase in frequency of our vibratory rate and the energies available to us.

"I still live within the Celestial Spheres
around the Sun and Central Sun,
but now I AM centered here on Earth,
with the Earth being the center
of Violet Fire Activity in the Universe."
~ *Energy, Vibration and Consciousness*
of the Legions of Violet Fire Angels, Group Avatar

And I thought of the disappearance of friend Nancy's arthritic old cat. Even though the cat had been house bound for the last few years, it had totally vanished. Nancy searched far and wide, particularly since it was wearing one of her precious amethyst crystals in its collar! A year later, during one of our Earth Healing ceremonies, Nancy, with tears in her eyes, said the cat had danced before her. Glowing with life and tossing its head to show off the bright jewel, saying; *See! I took it with me!*

That night I attended a small hypnotherapy workshop, and during a past life regression, experienced my life as a woodsman. I had a big dog. Was the dog Heidi? I had not supported my wife and children, and she had taken the little ones back to town. At the end of my life there was a deathbed scene, and my wife was there to take care of me. From that lifetime I learned the significance of forgiveness.

January 24, 1994 ~ Her Body Will Not Be Found

Others also are not questioning Heidi's disappearance. Rather are they swept by chills and thrills. Have we all not been reading and talking and dreaming about such things for the last few years? And we humans, having finally realized that Ascension is a process, can only wonder at Heidi's unfathomable demonstration. I ask, in the Light of Divine Discernment, how may I view Heidi's disappearance? Telepathically, words flow through my mind:

Heidi's disappearance may be used as a trigger, an activation in the minds of those who are ready to question the old beliefs and ways they have held so long, and which reflect the ways and beliefs of the mass consciousness. Heidi's disappearance shall be as an activation to their inner knowing. Heidi's disappearance was not of itself planned for this, but it may be used as such. And her body will not be found, for her body does not exist upon this Earth plane. Her vibratory rate was raised, was quickened as you would term it, in a manner that caused a transmutation of her cells, and it no longer exists in the realm of matter. Why, you ask, is this so? Because dear child, it is.

Do you question why the leaves unfold in spring?
Or why they fall at summer's end?
Then why do you question your beloved's passing

when her time had come?
For she is Angel in dog form and Angels too
must be about their Father's Business.
And when the Bird Tribe called to her ~ she came.

January 25, 1994 ~ The Beam of Light

I had not paid a great deal of attention to the footprints near the pines at the time, I had just noted the strangeness. But ever since Jim's comment, I keep thinking about them. Now, as I look through my bedroom window towards that spot, wondering, *how did you do it Heidi?* I had a momentary vision of Heidi ~ *walking in the moonlight, and pausing where the footsteps ended, and a small beam or tube, a pillar of light was upon her, about five or six times her height, and just her size.* And I understood, in a single instant, how this beam of light had allowed the acceleration of her bodily parts until she had spun, evaporated, dissolved, merged ~ until she had flowed into the next dimension. Heidi transitioned from third dimension, to be born again into a higher frequency, a higher level or plane of existence. Heidi vanished from the denseness of this physical expression, and was translated or transmuted into an alternate reality, just as whole tribes have done before her. One could indeed say that she was beamed up, spun or lifted ~ *ascended* into the next dimension. Heidi didn't consciously do anything, when the moment came, she switched screens and experienced rapture. Heidi Quantum Jumped! She went from particle-function expression in the world of form to wave-function Consciousness in the world of Spirit.

By her demonstration, Heidi made a reality of my beliefs, an example of what can be. *Oh, how I love you Heidi!*

> "Regarding our reality in Spirit,
> where we exist as an Eternal Flame
> with no form whatsoever,
> which has chosen to anchor itself
> through many embodiments on Earth."
> ~ *Beloved Mighty Victory, Ascended and Free*

January 28, 1994 ~ The Rose

I began my morning meditation with the Group Avatar Breathing Statement for the month; 'Inbreathing and Absorbing the Violet Flame of Forgiveness, Integration and Spiritual Release into Freedom ~ Expanding and Projecting the Violet Flame of Forgiveness, Integration and Spiritual Release into Freedom'. After repeating this several times, words flowed into my mind:

And this is the Forcefield offered by Sananda (the Garden of Sananda). Energized by the love of one who craves Ascension (author). Magnetized by this one into the reality of the physical realm, the Father/Mother God dance the Crystal Violet Flame of Forgiveness into Being. And it is anchored through the heart of one in embodiment, into the physical realm where it shall establish a new frequency, a new Law of Attraction to which ones shall come who would be cleansed.

And upon the Ascension spot shall grow a perfect rose. Not within the physical dimension, but on the etheric, and yet its perfume may permeate the dimensions and create awareness in the ones who choose to honor the departure of Heidi the Beloved. For she is a great Angel, and her Presence shall ever be around this place as long as the one she loves remains in form.

And Heidi is the central core, the unifying principle of this band of Angels that she is. And from her heart there bursts a thousand radiations of crystal light, and each an angel which may expand or retract as the occasion calls. And within her heart, within the heart of this pulsating Light that you term Heidi, the angels nestle in oneness, ever ready, ever ready, ever ready to electrify their thoughts and project in unison a thousand, or ten thousand units individualized for that at hand ~ or banded as a wave of light to bless the land. A crystalline Violet Forcefield of perfection directed by their leader, the one who stands Earth based and knows this truth.

Heidi shall not communicate directly, one on one. She prefers to release the individualization that she knew on Earth and breathe her essence into your mind as words for you to grasp. It was only her love for you that kept her anchored in a realm that was not home to her. And now she has expanded to her full degree and would not retract her essence ever more.

"Heidi was Light slowed down!" ~ William Henry

NOTE: March 2024, as we go to print. In this month's *Ascended and Free* journal is the phrase, *Imagine that the Violet Fire itself is finally finding a Home on Earth, within Ascended and Free Humanity.* These words seem strikingly relevant to the transmission above, where there is mention of the Violet Fire being anchored into this realm.

Regarding that rose! I did wonder about it. And forgot about it. Many years later, I bought a beautiful ceramic tiled steppingstone of a rose for the garden. I didn't know where to put it, so for several months it just sat under the Pine tree near the garage. By this time Tiggy was nearly 17 years old and when a friend was admiring it, I commented that it was rather like a memorial plaque for Tiggy ~ and was instantly rather embarrassed by such a thought. Anyway, I eventually felt the need to move it, and without thinking, carried it past the labyrinth and placed it on Heidi's Ascension spot. Amazingly, several more months passed before I remembered the above meditation when I was told; *and on the Ascension spot shall grow a perfect rose!* I assumed that the Rose was now so well established in the spirit realms that it could manifest in form!

February 2, 1994 ~ Logic vs. Frequency

I was not consciously thinking of Heidi as I called for my highest guides and teachers, in order that I may know them more clearly. And they say:

We are Devic in essence, as are you. Angelic, as is Heidi. And you and Heidi are one essence at Source, but for the purpose of assisting this Earth have you split ~ and she works with you from her devic essence. And yes, it is what you term your twin angel, a portion of which, a minute portion formed as Gretel (Heidi's mother). And another part of itself, did it project as Heidi. And they were not the same essence, Heidi and Gretel, although they came, they emanated from the one. But your fingers and your toes are very different are they not? Although they are one at source. And so it is with these ones that come to you as dogs. They carry a different vibration or frequency because they come from a different portion, or part of the whole. Their purpose is different. Gretel's was unconditional Love, the Spirit of Harmlessness. Heidi was to anchor the frequency of the Violet Flame in the area or location where you have stationed yourself. And so she bore, or carried the frequency of forgiveness, which you find hard to understand because you are rationalizing and trying to think logically, what does this mean?

You cannot equate logic with frequency. Accept that she has played her part in the scheme, or unfoldment of the divine plan. She has executed her mission with exact aplomb, and she was called home, as you would term it, at the exact moment that her mission was complete. It had to do with your own understanding as well as the timing in your Earth plane. The timing was in place, and it was only for your understanding to expand and allow her to be released. Thus it was the expansion of your own awareness, the quotient of your own Light frequency, that pulled the trigger and allowed her freedom, the integration of her essence released to Spiritual Freedom.

And you were guided of course, to attend that workshop (the hypnotherapy one). And now you wonder who does the guiding!? Your own High Self, or us who speak now as your guides? Well dear one, it was us, for we were working in close affinity with Heidi, the essence of Heidi, whom we were ready to receive back into our circle of oneness. For she is one with us at the core of her essence.

You cannot hope to understand exactly of what we speak. But know that Heidi, in the pureness of her True Self, is one with the circle of guides who speak to you now. And because she has been so close to you, it will allow us to work more closely with you. This also was a part of her plan, to bring forth a closer connection with your guides because she had been in a physical form with you.

And so Heidi has created, or anchored this Pillar of Violet Flame. Attaching you might say, your realm to ours through Violet Fire, by a Flame or Frequency of Violet Fire. And it is for us to work through this Violet Flame rather than for you to worry about it. But you may draw upon this Violet Flame and direct it and center yourself within its core and call for Divine Mercy, Compassion and Forgiveness to be drawn into your realm and directed where you send it.

Regarding 'the expansion of my own awareness', I was of course most eager to know exactly what I had done or learned to accomplish this! What had I been doing or reading or watching?! I couldn't remember a thing and had to accept that it was probably yet another process, a variation of the 'last straw' effect.

February 4, 1994 ~ The Great Rays

There were some aspects of this Violet Fire and Heidi that I couldn't quite grasp, or maybe it was just that I couldn't quite believe. Friend Shumala was visiting, and I asked her to ask Sananda, a Great Being or Forcefield of Light and Goodness, to help me. He came right away, and Shumala relayed what she was seeing in her mind's eye; "As soon as you mentioned Heidi's name, his head went back, and he's laughing. He looks like that dolphin over there (a poster on the wall). He's LAUGHING, and he says; *That was quite a trick wasn't it!* And he shows me ~ he's holding Heidi, and she's looking up at him with 'that look'. Her eyes to his eyes. It's like this wonderful cosmic joke." Sananda speaks through Shumala;

And I would say to you, dearest Angel One ~ from the Angels have all of you come. And it is difficult to process it in the thinking mind, so we ask for you to go to the heart and feel this as you very often do, rather than trying to figure it all out. Realize that this great tapestry you have woven for your life, was all decided way before you came into body. And that there were agreements among all of the souls involved, and we would include all of the souls of these beings known to some as dogs ~ and known to those of you who know as the energy Light of different aspects of the Godhead.

And we will say it in this way, that for you to have a complete energy vibration here in this particular place that we chose together (the Garden of Sananda), that it was necessary for you to have Energy Rays from all corners of the Universe. If you look at this place, and you feel this place, you will understand that all the highest vibrations from all the Rays are here. In a way, as you look at the Great Central Sun and the Rays that have come from that, and seemingly separated ~ all were to be anchored here. And this was an agreement that was made ever so long ago. Truly aeons ago. Actually when you left the Garden of Lemuria and there was seemingly a spiral into more density on the Earth. But you kept that promise in the chamber of your heart, and now is the time for the return if you will. Understand that you are recreating the energy of the gardens of Lemuria here.

When I first came to this garden in the early summer of 1985, there was nothing in it. No flowers, no shrubs. The birds did not even fly over it. Slowly it came to life. Seven years passed and I was guided to start making flower and mineral essences, the Sananda Ascension Essences. I was also very aware that Great Rays were anchoring through an area I called the Fairy Ring. First to come was the Spirit of Beauty, followed by the Spirit of Peace and then, the Spirit of Wisdom and the Spirit of Service. But so much was happening at that time, on all levels, that I rather lost track of what was going on and what Rays came next! To continue:

So this Blessed One known to you as Heidi was an aspect of the Violet Ray, an ingredient that was very much needed, and in her so-called leaving, of course she does not take that with her, but it has been very powerfully anchored here. And the vision that you had of the thousand points of light from her ~ understand that her central being now, is showering down ~ and picture that as I spoke of the ripples that you have caused, that have really been reverberating around the world ~ that which is the essence of Blessed Heidi also reverberates into those places. If you would picture a shower of stars into all these places where your light has reverberated, then the light of this Blessed One brings the Violet Flame to all those places.

It is in a way, a completion of the puzzles. Not that you are not a complete light in the eyes of the Mother/Father God, but in order for you to anchor the power of the work that you came to do, there was a cooperative effort if you will, a returning together of souls of Light. Much easier sometimes with those who are in the animal kingdom, for they have this pure light with none of the human complications. More difficult when it is star brothers and sisters who are shuffling here and there, and in varying degrees of remembering and then forgetting why they came.

I asked about the Ascension Vortex as we are calling it. Is it just where Heidi stood, or is it an expandable vortex? Did the Pines have something to do with it? The well? The crystal? Was it a special energy spot before or after Heidi's ascension?

Yes. It is the trees and the crystals (the garden and the house are filled with crystals). And if you were to look down from above, you would see an interesting pattern, the grid that you have created (unconsciously) with the crystals. There is more than one expandable vortex here on the property. The entire piece of property is of course itself an energy vortex, and then there are these little places of even higher frequency within this place.

People often walked around the garden, stopping to gasp at various places where they feel an intensification of energies, ley lines or whatever, and I feel nothing! One day I asked about this. How could this be? What were people experiencing? Immediately within my mind, I saw the entire space enclosed or held within a vast etheric Star Tetrahedron and understood that different people were picking up on different parts or aspects of this, whereas I, because I live within this frequency, feel nothing different.

Many years later still, when I (and the dogs), were facilitating Animal Communication playdays here at Sananda, we would do an exercise where people could invite their own animal to come, in their imagination, and explore the house or the garden and give us their perceptions of what they saw and felt. Many times people, who knew nothing of the above, would invite their horse, and they would see in their mind's eye, that the horses were walking around the garden in specific geometric patterns that on occasion included the labyrinth. And sometimes the neighboring horses, standing silhouetted up on the hill, would join us in our thoughts, and show us a lighted gridwork of energy across the land, a sort of celebration of Light and Sound created during our different gatherings, which often included drumming and chanting ~ events they seemed to much enjoy watching.

February 7, 1994 ~ Fusion

I forget the lead into the following meditation. Undoubtedly I had been thinking about Heidi and how she 'did it', or rather ~ how *did* she do it? And the thought came; *after the integration, when one has reached the point of integration between spirit and matter, then there is fusion ~ and this is the point of ascension.* I wasn't sure about that word fusion! At that time, I had never heard anyone talk about fusion! And anyway, how does this relate to Heidi?

Heidi had reached the point of integration, the balance between spirit and matter, and at this point of balance, integration becomes fusion, allowing entry into a higher frequency. But there is also at this time (the time we are all in now, the present moment), the need to allow re-entry into the plane you leave, and the process is not complicated by this requirement. But it must be understood that this is not a case of release which may be termed escape. It is a point of growth, of ascension, that you may accomplish more easily and readily your purpose upon Earth. And it is only for those who understand fully that this is not an escape but a blessing of Divine Grace, who shall be allowed at this point in time, at this present moment, to attain their ascension, and return in their Light Bodies, in accordance with their original Divine Plan. For there is need of ones, great need of such ones, and we shall assist you all we may. And for your part to assist us, lighten your body, the physical body, hold true to your focus of Enlightenment for all, and expect a miracle.

"When the first humans still lived in the bosom of the Eternal and were in constant communion with it, nothing was hidden. The divine life in which they were immersed was their sole and perfect source of knowledge. If you want to regain some of this primordial knowledge, you must commune with the universe, the ocean of Cosmic Light. Until you succeed in reaching this higher state of consciousness termed communion *or fusion*, you cannot know it." ~ Omraam Mikhaël Aïvanhov

February 9, 1994 ~ The Song of Freedom

I was thinking about Heidi. I was thinking about her restlessness in the evenings. For the past two or three months, about the middle of the evening, just when I was ready to sit-stay, Heidi would start wandering around. She would stand and stare aimlessly into space. She would wander into the kitchen and just stand there. I would pick her up and hold her, and she would relax for a few minutes, resting her head under my chin, and then she would want down, to continue her wanderings. This was in no way a dementia type of wandering. So I would put her outside, and joyfully she would bound into the night, and because it was so cold I would insist she come in again very soon. Now I wondered ~ had she known what was coming?

And it was at an atomic cellular level that Heidi's name was called. Not in her conscious mind did she hear this call, but in the very atoms of her cellular make up was this call heard. And it was the excitement that was felt at this level, the knowing that soon they would receive their spiritual release into freedom. Not trapped were they but bound by love to hold the form of one you held most dear, and excitement ~ anticipation, are the words with which we would equate their feeling. And it was in the evening that they felt this pressure, or buildup of energies, singing their song, calling them home. For it was a buildup. As a mighty symphonic sound that rises to a crescendo of crashing cymbals, and when that point was reached, their time had come. And the one for whom they held that form was powerless almost to resist ~ the stirrings of her heart would be your translation or understanding. But it was far deeper, or more encompassing than that. It was the Song of Freedom that sang to every part and particle of her molecular make up, her structure. And this blessed one answered Freedom's call with Divine Integrity and Grace.

And she it is who dances
in the Flame of the Mother/Father God,
in union with their Cosmic Heart of Oneness.

And she will call to you, this one. In the same manner that she was called, will she call to you. And by 'she' understand that this includes a vast array of Beingness to which you are ~ affiliated is the only word we can muster at this time. And when your name is called, it will reverberate throughout your Being with a knowingness that may not be withstood; and you will be drawn, as Heidi was drawn, to be where it is you are to be. And so it is with each, when their moment of freedom, their moment of spiritual release into Freedom is upon them, they shall hear a call and they shall follow this Call of Service as a wave follows the call of the ocean.

As to the timing, this may not be given, because the timing is not set in a linear time frame. The timing is Cosmic. In a Cosmic reference table this event has already happened, this event is in effect even as we speak. In a linear time frame, it is adjustable. It is on a sliding scale of many dependables. It is your Self who adjusts the balance, aided of course, by the many variables in which you live, by which you are guided and upon which the very rhythm of your world depends, God bless. ~ We are the Brotherhood of Light. The Brotherhood of Love. The Brotherhood of the Violet Flame. Sisters in Oneness, Brothers by Law.

March 2, 1994 ~ Angel That She Is

A letter has arrived from Jamala, otherwise known as Frank Babcock. A dear friend who has not visited recently, but the last time he departed, he returned to the house after making his farewells, murmuring, *I didn't say goodbye to Heidi.* He stood beside her, not touching her physically, but communing at some deep level only he and Heidi knew. I wrote to tell him of Heidi's ascension. He replied;

Two days ago when I was nearly complete with my morning meditation, I was visited by one who is recently ascended. I refer of course to Heidi. She appeared in lovely Light. I sensed her wings and golden halo. She wishes to help me in my work, to be part of our ongoing attempt to awaken the sleeping Lightworkers. Her energy is so loving and sweet. She has reunited with Gretel (her mother). She reminded me this morning that I needed to send this information to you and is looking over my shoulder as I write. She loves you so very much and is so grateful to you for looking after her and Tiggy and Loreli. She tells me she is in touch with you but wanted for me to pass on her feelings to you. I welcome her blessed assistance, and feel honored and loved that she would come to me;

I was deeply touched to read of Heidi's Ascension.
Tears came to my eyes.
Not tears of sadness but tears of Joy,
of Celebration,
of the perfection of Heidi.
I felt her Joy, her Joyous Being
And I was blessed ~ and blessed her,
Angel that she is ~ in the Oneness of God.
The Christ Consciousness Vibration,
The Divine Love.
~ Jamala

March 4, 1994 ~ The Ascension Vortex

The county animal shelter telephoned. Had I found my little lost dog? I had forgotten I called them that mystic morning nearly six weeks ago. My heart wasn't in it. It was old programming. Guilt, that made me do it. Fear of people asking whether I had done everything possible to find her. So now I was taken by surprise. *Er, um, ah ~ NO! She, um ~ she DIED!* I blurted. It was the first time I had said that. They expressed their condolences, and I thanked them. A couple of days later I received a notice in the mail from this same shelter. Already I had forgotten the phone call, and supposed it was a routine flyer asking for money or drawing attention to a fund raiser. Not so. It was a touching little note that said, "Please accept our heartfelt sympathy in the loss of your pet. Know that we understand and share in your sorrow." And there was a poignant little sketch of a big scruffy dog hugging a small and grieving teddy bear. I still have it.

The previous year I had been guided to start making flower essences, vibrational remedies, from the garden flowers. Minerals too, were to be part of the thirty-two-bottle set of Sananda Ascension Essences. Up until now, I had always set the bowl of water in which they lay, at the feet of a statue of Francis of Assisi, in an area I call the central vortex. Whatever essence is to be made is brought to my attention by direct inner knowing, and I never know when this will be. Now, suddenly, I am aware that I am to make the essence of Danburite, a brilliant diamond like clear quartz crystal to be placed in a bowl of water in the Heidi Ascension Vortex, at the same time of month that she departed. Danburite ~ *for remembrance and expression of Light Being, an inter-dimensional connecting link.*

The following month I would be guided to make an essence of Pine Root ~ not only to be made from a pine whose roots extend into this vortex area, but at the exact same time of night that Heidi ascended. And by the light of a full moon, which burst from a storm filled sky and shone brightly through the dripping, rain drenched branches. I dug and washed the little piece of root to the steady tone of a friend playing her African clay drum. Somewhat ironically, Pine Root is for grounding ~ in the middle of an Ascension Vortex!

March 6, 1994 ~ Definition of Ascension

For the purpose of explaining to others, I have asked for a simple definition on what exactly is Ascension?

Ascension is a process. The evolutionary course of humankind is peaked, you might say, in physical embodiment to allow an influx of Christed energy, or Light from the higher realms as you term them, realms of a higher frequency than the one wherein you dwell as we term it, that shall accelerate the vibratory patterns or rate of this physical form. And what you do to allow this, is your choice ~ evolution as you contemplate it in a linear fashion, that is. But evolution as we see it, on the spiral dance of life. And so, this acceleration of your bodily parts shall take place regardless, because of the rays or energies with which you are bombarded or highlighted. But you yourself may greatly accelerate this process by your own intention, and by means of supporting this phenomenon. And by support, we mean anything that assists that physical part of yourself to accept more light and merge into this lighter or higher frequency.

And yes, there comes a point of fusion, in which at an atomic level, the light within is ignited. The light within each atom is ignited by outside forces you would think of it ~ for even your intent in this case, is an outside force to the atom itself.

And so, we have these ignited atoms throughout your being, sparkling, burning, blazing, and once ignited they may not be extinguished. Much as you may not squelch an electric fire with water, so shall they burn on everlasting. And as you continue in your devotions to this process, so may the molecules be ignited by the atoms, and the cells by the molecules. It is a process of infiltration. The atoms themselves were ignited by fusion, and then the process of infiltration continues. Until one day, your whole being glows from the inside out, lit by the radiance of the Christ Light shining forth from the very core of your Being. And then shall the physical world hold no boundaries for you. For one of Light interpenetrates at will the dimensions and walls of limitation that have been built by the mind and held in place by the beliefs of a critical mass. And so, when there are enough beings doing this, these thought patterns shall change as realization dawns and awareness grows, that these walls of limitation are simply a web, a pattern of thought structures held together by the belief of the individual.

How to sum it up in a few words, eh? You did not expect a dissertation! Just a couple of sentences you wanted. And so; Ascension is an evolutionary process in which the physical body becomes fused with its counterpart of Light.

And when we talk about the physical matter being accelerated into its counterpart Light body, we do not necessarily mean just the physical form of the human being. We are referring to all physical matter on earth, indeed, the Earth herself. For those who do not take their bodies with them, what do you suppose happens to them, dear one? They remain on earth do they not? (The bodies). And so, they shall be transformed none the less, these physical parts. Whether the consciousness of the human is in them or not, they shall be transformed. A process or happening that is inevitable whether you believe it or not. And for those who do not believe, it shall not happen in their physical embodiment but after they have departed such. And for those who do believe ~ this process may be greatly accelerated.

And I was moved to make the following decree:
*I ask for all consciousness at an atomic level to be ignited.
That this Flame of Light that I send forth from my heart,
shall crack the codes that kept the Christ Light sealed,
and allow it now to blaze forth in full glory ~ creating a fusion,
igniting the matter around and in which it dwells.*

March 7, 1994 ~ Blanket of Light

On the strength of Jamala's letter and the fact that he is obviously seeing Heidi as an angel, and I am not seeing her at all ~ I ask for a symbol or way that I can think of Heidi. Nothing. Nada! Slightly despondent, I just keep breathing. Eventually I am asked how I feel. Suddenly I am aware that I feel absolutely, joyfully wonderful!

*Heidi is holding a forcefield or blanket of Light around you
as you held her so often.*

And I felt a love so overpowering, so all-encompassing and overwhelming, that tears of emotional gratitude rolled down my face. If ever Heidi was cold or wet, or just not feeling so good, I would hold her tight, often wrapped in a big towel or blanket. And now she was doing the same for me.

> "As the mountains are round about Jerusalem,
> so the Lord is round about his people
> from henceforth even forever." ~ *Psalm 125*

And I remembered how Heidi nurtured and loved me while still in physical form. One day when my mind was in turmoil over misunderstandings with a dear friend, I called for assistance in transmuting this mindless conflict, to be filled again with joy and enthusiasm ~ Heidi came into my lap and beamed her love into my eyes.

Heidi would share her love with you. The purest Love of the Father, the Creator. The Love that permeates all Spirit and holds the World together, your world and mine. For Heidi is of the Mother, the Spirit Love ~ and through her it might shine, and by her it may be directed. And she directs it to you, for it is you with whom she came to interact. Solely at first, but as her mission reached fulfillment and trust in herself o'erflowed, was she able to reach further with her love, and draw a larger circle around herself. And from her Self extend her aura ~ some might say, her circle of awareness, that others exist who may be integrated without threat to herself, into her world.

And so the circle grows, ever energizing greater truths and other worlds, other realities ~ with ever the need for greater strength and security at the center point. And Heidi would remind you that she stands with you at the hub. The angel that she truly is stands with you. As do the Angels of the Lord, the Angelic Kingdom, the realms and legions of the Angel Ones stand with you and around you, above and below. Call on them, honor them, accept their love and ministrations through the gentle one that came to you in furry form. We love you ever and always, Angels in Light, Angels of Light, Angels of Dawn ~ the Brotherhood of Light.

> "My Gift to you is Love, that Love which I want you to feel.
> Personally, I as an individual intelligence,
> entirely apart from my Official Status,
> send you daily my Love to warm your heart and soul,
> and that Love from Me to you is as your eternal friend.
> Accept it now and use it."
> ~ *Lord Maitreya in Bridge to Freedom 1955*

March 8, 1994 ~ Fountain of Youth

I am enfolded in the radiance of Heidi's love and in the Flame of Cosmic Grace. I breathe in Light. I feed my cells upon this Light. I AM my Light body. I breathe the Light into my cells, into my molecules, and this Light floods and fills my form, surrounding the atoms at the core of each particle that I AM. And the pressure from this Light that I breathe, with which I feed my cells, is the trigger that opens the atoms to release their treasure ~ *and then there is fusion*. And this fusion has taken place within my mind; it has only to manifest, to percolate through into the physical, and then it shall BE ~ as I AM.

The atoms one might say, are activated to open to the Light by the infiltration that comes from my intent. They have been on alert for some time, and now comes the moment of Truth when they are triggered to release their secret living Light and flood my being with this Flame of Eternal Substance ~ the Fountain of Youth it has been termed.

And it is this Fountain that is within mine self, within each and every atom that holds my shape in form. And this Fountain of Youth is the secret to youth eternal, limitless abundance and physical perfection. And I have found wherein it dwells, and now it is for me to activate these fountains and keep them flowing. And when I have learned the secret, they will be maintenance free for ever more. I paused in my meditation, in my mind. And where my own mind paused, a greater Mind continued:

And so, what is the secret to activate these fountains and keep the pressure at full command? The secret at first may be termed work ~ on all levels. On all levels. And after that, when the work is done, they shall flow in freedom and unity ever more. Meanwhile they have some turbulence to pierce. They have been held at bay, suppressed so long, it is almost as though they must burst through a crust that has accumulated. But the doors have been opened, it is only the outer shell that needs to be removed. The sealed doors have been activated, drawn back, unveiled. God bless ~ we are the Brotherhood of Love, The Brotherhood of Light, and Heidi is our spokesperson this glorious day.

And we shall help you cleanse this crust and grime.
Each time you sit to breathe the Light, we shall be there.
Each time you lie to sleep, we shall enfold you with our prayer.

*Each time you note the joyous thing ~ of beauty, sound,
of thought or deed ~ a little more shall be chipped away.
Ascension is truly a fusion. A feeling of Freedom and Unity,
harmonizing within the core of every part of your inner self.*

"The balancing of Freedom and Unity
is the Universal Law that governs process."
~ *Group Avatar*

March 10, 1994 ~ The Furry Fairy

Just as I sat to meditate, Tiggy came to sit beside me. Darling Tiggy, my furry fairy. Now she is asleep, but I ask if she would speak. And she says;

I am angel also. The fairy ones are Angelic, forget not this. And I am resting in the light that Heidi holds around me too. She blesses us (Tiggy and Loreli), and thanks us for our love to her when she was here. And now she holds us as a mother holds her babe in arms, and cares for us, and watches over us in all we do. We feel her joy and love ~ and as it seeps and penetrates more deeply into our living forms, we shall express that part of her that is true Love.

March 10, 1994 ~ The Cloud of Peace

The dogs love it when I meditate! And the above, when Tiggy came to sit beside me, reminded me of another time, long ago, when Heidi came to join me as I sat in contemplation. Such a beautiful day; I was meditating outside amid the pine trees, when a truck went by on the small country road at the bottom of the garden, letting off a loud bang which made me jump. A moment later, Heidi came quietly and sat beside me. That scared you too Heidi, didn't it?

Yes, I didn't like that bang, it shattered my cloud of peace. Loud noises that come from nowhere, I don't like them. They shatter the peaceful energies around me. And I love the beautiful cloud of peace that is around me. Does Tiggy have one? A cloud of peace? It is growing, she has a little thin faint one sometimes. But mine is deep and lush and warm. I love my cloud of peace. And Gretel? Did Gretel have one? Of course Gretel had one, it was so voluminous it bumped into everything.

Everyone got touched by Gretel's cloud of peace. Mine is for me, and my special friends. Tiggy likes snuggling into it. It is pink and green and blue and gold, and all stuck together with light. Shiny white light.

March 16, 1994 ~ The State of I AMNESS

Sitting in the sun on the front steps I have called for the presence of Francis of Assisi, known for his great love of animals and birds. He once told me, through Shumala, that not one animal passes from this existence to the next without him there to greet it. And he had shown her pictures of him greeting each and every factory chicken as they passed through the slaughterhouses. It made her cry. Now it occurred to me to wonder if he had greeted Heidi in her transition. And how had she felt, I wondered? How had she experienced this transition? This Ascension? I called for the essence of beloved Heidi to come and tell me, to share with me, what she had experienced that precious night ~ *and I (Sananjaleen), felt a great and wondrous warmth, as from the sun. But this warmth was all through and around my body, to the very core of my being. It was as though every cell and molecule of my existence was bathed with an incredibly warm, all powerful and loving energy. I could have stayed there forever, but before I had a chance to truly bask in the glory of this, I experienced every part and particle of my self expanding out and out and out ~ until I filled all space. And there was nothing left of me but pure conscious awareness of THAT I AM.*

> "In our Ascended and Free Consciousness,
> we live in a Realm of warmth, love, peace and beauty,
> 'The Kingdom of Heaven within'!"
> *~ Ascended and Free*

By surrounding me, permeating me with her higher frequency, the frequency of where she currently was, Heidi enabled me to attain that for myself. She 'raised me up'! When I had gathered myself together again, I asked her to put in words what she herself had experienced, please. She was very sweet, very gentle, and I was grateful that she spoke from her Heidi-dog perspective, rather than an infinite point of consciousness.

I had to go out. I just had to go out. And I was drawn to that place. And as I stood ~ I felt a great warmth, an incredible Ray of Light around me. Greater than any ray of sunlight that ever warmed my body did this Light feel. And it warmed me, to the very core of my deepest existence. The warmth was within me, and I felt myself expanding. I felt myself separating and growing vaster in all directions, until I experienced myself simply as my own thought. And it was as though I was back where I had always been. It did not seem that I had ever left this state of consciousness. And it is this state of I AMNESS with which I am enabled to surround you, to surround Jamala, and feed you my love. I cannot explain how it is done, I simply think my love around you, and so it is. A projection of my love for you.

Heidi ~ empty of self,
a state of pure consciousness
attaining the infinite field of possibility.

"A direct transmission of Light
taken to God Consciousness."
~ Dan Winter

Was Francis there to meet me, you ask? It was as though he had never left my side. It was not so much that he was waiting there for me to return, as the experience that I was the one who was awakening to my own return. Awakening, returning from a dream of being away.

"For a mass to travel faster than light, it would simply have to achieve wholeness with the universal structure, which is not a question of speed, but of identification with form. It is a matter of becoming one with the light. Identification with light is the key to transcending form and speed."
~ *Saryon Michael White*

And how do I view my life with you? The one you call beloved Heidi. I smile at her, that dear one. So joyful in her expression of love for you. I thank her for being that part of me that dwelt on Earth and took advantage of every occasion to observe and feel and learn and know the ways of physicality. She was at first perturbed, and very lost to find herself upon that plane. And then you came, and all was clear to her. Her path of purpose unfurled before her, so to speak. And she did not consciously hurt herself, to move into your presence, as you have often wondered. But we would say, she was given a little push for this to occur ~ by us, who for the sake of terminology may be termed her higher selves.

Of course I shall continue to work with you. And it is not necessary for you to know my presence, for my presence may not actively be around you. It shall be as emanations of my Love, surrounding and holding you in that Forcefield for you to draw upon in your daily work, in your daily growth.

May 1, 1994 ~ Was and Is!

In the Group Avatar journal there is talk on Infinity Consciousness, and a description of the release of the Suspended Breath. It sums up Heidi's exodus most exactly with the words; *'and what was, suddenly is no more'*! A later journal explained.

> "In this suspended Breath of Purity,
> you began to approach that single Cosmic Moment
> when 'what was suddenly is no more',
> and in its place is the Divine Plan." ~ *Group Avatar*

And from the great Bulgarian spiritual master Peter Deunov (Beinso Douno 1864 -1944), in reference to the New Era, the 6th Race, the time of Ascension we are in now:

> "Within it, death will exist no more.
> When the time comes to depart,
> one will dematerialize, will become invisible."

May 5, 1994 ~ Others Did It Too

Friend Star has phoned, from Advanced Tachyon Technologies in California. I have sent several people 'the Heidi story so far'. Star said she was reading it for the fourth or fifth time. At first she questioned the disappearance of the body, but in meditation she too had seen Heidi surrounded in a great light, and questioned no more. And in telling the Heidi story, I am hearing of other dogs and cats of her exact age group 'disappearing', as well as can be remembered, that same day.

The weekend after Heidi went, I phoned a neighbor I had been planning to contact for the last few years. She was moving that very day, and upon hearing the Heidi story said that her own dog had also 'vanished' last weekend. Her little dog was old and arthritic, and could not possibly have wandered far, and although Sally had been given in her own meditations the exact same words as I; *that the body would not be found*, it had not fully registered in her consciousness until this moment.

Then came a visitor from Colorado to our Earth Healing group, a special ceremony in which we placed small glass bowls of water on a carefully chosen cloth on the floor, and everyone roamed the house selecting whatever drew their attention to bring to the circle ~ a crystal, an ornament, a stuffed animal. Each would then say a few words regarding their particular concerns for the week and place a drop or two of a flower essence into the water as we offered our love and support to the various Animal and Nature Kingdoms in need. The little longhaired Dachshunds loved this ceremony! They would wander among the treasures, taking small licks from each bowl, and on one or two memorable occasions they found edibles treats! This visitor was also treated to the Heidi story. Suddenly, she remembered hearing her neighbors talk of their old cat. A cat who had never left, nor could it easily get out of the apartment in which it had lived for 17 years. Gone! Nowhere could a trace of it be found. The same weekend, she knew.

And then there was Heidi's friend Star, a most beautiful and gentle black and white longhaired cat whom the dogs and I used to cat-care while his people were away. Had Star just vanished, his family would have been greatly distressed and spent much time searching for him. On the morning of Heidi's departure, Star woke early and cried. His human scrambled out of bed and picked him up. The elderly Star jumped from her arms, a thing he had never done before, twisting himself in such a manner that he had to be taken to the vet, and given release from his physical body.

Heidi's story also brought peace of mind to those who honored that this is what had happened to their own animals, though many years ago. One friend gave a very similar account of their elderly dog barking and bouncing around late one snowy night, until finally, her husband let it out. They too, had been left with paw prints that just stopped, and no dog to be found. They assumed a wind had blown across the tracks, and her husband berated himself still for letting the old dog out unattended.

And a young man attending a workshop I was giving regarding the Ascension Essences, could hardly wait to ask; *So if they disappear, they could also APPEAR, couldn't they?!* For him it clarified a great mystery he and his wife had experienced that winter. They had rented a small cabin in the woods, some distance from any road or other housing, snow and ice lay deep around. One morning, a small kitten had miraculously appeared in their kitchen!

Now I understand, that as I had laid the structure or foundation for Heidi to transmute her physical being by sharing and declaring that she would, so has she done the same for me by doing it. Show and tell! And in telling the story, so is the possibility of a new format being seeded into the minds of all who hear, laying the foundation for the possibility of 'miracles' to occur at any moment, as we all continue ever upward and inward on the spiral of Enlightenment ~ our return to Love and Grace, with full consciousness of That I AM. Not that all might wish to do as Heidi did, but all might wish for a body of Light that knows no pain and has no limitations.

And on the flip side of the coin, my dear neighbor, a horse veterinarian, and rider of some renown, remarked that it was a pity I had not looked for wing marks in the snow, for it was surely an owl that got her! Some owl. Heidi weighed 21 lbs. Google says owls can lift 4 lbs. Causing even more merriment, was the response of a well-known leading publisher of Ascension material who said, "How can you be sure she wasn't abducted?!"

And it wasn't just dogs and cats who were 'doing it'! After printing Heidi's story as a small, stapled booklet, the stories continued. Hermit Crabs were doing it too! I received a lovely note saying, "This email is prompted by my reading about the Ascension of your beautiful Heidi. Since last November I had a small hermit crab, and showered Hermie with love and light. A few weeks ago Hermie buried itself in the sand in a corner of the little terrarium in which it lived. I assumed that it was about to molt and exchange its shell for a larger one. I checked the corner occasionally to see if there was movement, but never spotted a difference in the small mound covering Hermie. Finally, I decided I should see how Hermie was doing underneath the pile of sand. To my surprise and joyful delight, there was absolutely no sign of my little crab or its shell. You are the first person to hear this anecdote. I have the strong feeling that Hermie ascended, through the unconditional caring and love it received. Could this be? *In Light and Love, Bob.*"

And then there was the Ascension of my friend Pilar's goldfish! At that time, Pilar lived in a small townhouse apartment with a goldfish in a little round bowl on the kitchen windowsill. This window did not open, it was an upstairs apartment with no way for stray cats or other animals to enter. Only Pilar was in the house, and one morning ~ the goldfish was not present! Where do you start looking for a missing goldfish?! It was a bare bowl with nowhere to hide! Mystified and baffled, Pilar puzzled and puzzled. She knew the Heidi story well, but our minds are not programmed to jump to such conclusions. Eventually, she told me of the dilemma, and I promptly declared her goldfish had obviously 'done a Heidi'. Of course! Truth flooded her soul, and joy and harmony restored to her being.

And in 2010, nearly fifteen years later, I received an email from someone who had heard the Heidi Story, saying; "I have just experienced my cat 'vanishing' from her red tent where she slept on my bed, between 1.30 am and 5 am. Please tell me what you know of this happening. How often does it happen and how I can follow her?" I think my response was not at all helpful!

And in March 2021, a friend sent me an email that her Bunny had just ascended! Complete with photo of footprints in the snow, footprints that just stopped! What did this mean to her? "I think it means that our ascension is nigh. Very close to the finish line." And Miriam (Reverend Absurd) herself *almost* returned to Spirit very soon after that. Seemingly it was a case of *access denied,* and she was returned to Earth!

May 6, 1994 ~ Angels

I have invoked the angels, and although I do not see her, I am sensing Heidi's presence and love. The overwhelming and all-encompassing love that I have come to expect and know when I call for her to be with me. Today I am hearing her angelic name; *Haloa a'Ha, Haloa a'Ha*. Very soft, so soft and rhythmic. So very soft and gentle. And although Heidi would not step to the fore, her angel companions always take a half step back as it were, to give her preference in administering her love to me.

June 5, 1994 ~ The Bondage of Love

Sitting between the pines in the early morning sun, I ask Lady Omega and Omnibus (my current guides, whom I vaguely understood as Great Cosmic Beings from the Central Sun), how is it that Heidi could ascend as she did, without consciously doing all the things we humans do in our endeavors to raise the light quotient within our cells. And Lady Omega says:

This was prearranged. When one agrees to come in a body such as that of an animal, where it is known there will not be need of conscious awareness for this development, it is prearranged. The body is set on automatic so to speak. They are set on automatic, that their vehicle will reach a certain vibratory rate at a certain time, in accordance in this case, with your own vibratory rate. And so dear one, it was a direct reflection of the light quotient as you call it, of light energy received and activated by your own cells, that triggered her mechanism in allowing her to go. In releasing her from this form of bondage, which was of course, a bondage of Love.

And I wonder whether sweet Tiggy will go the same way. And I feel them smile. And Loreli? I am only aware of her dancing with me along my path, it is too early yet to think of Loreli leaving. And the thought comes to me that perhaps Tiggy will dissolve, will spin into a golden ball of light. In her ball of golden light that brought her from the fairy kingdoms. She didn't! At least, not in this dimension. Much later, I realized she probably did! I just couldn't see it.

January 1995 ~ The Game of Life

Heidi has been much on my mind lately, the beautiful fun things she did as a dog. She was so wonderful. Her coat was so glorious. She was so genteel! So refined! She bore such an air of nobility. An air that made it all the more implausible when she chased chickens, chewed all the crumble off an apple pie or rolled in horse poop. I recalled the time I opened the front door, and there was Heidi ~ a set of newborn baby bunnies stashed in a row inside her long jaws. The one nearest her nose was still alive and I rushed it to my neighbor, a nurse with two young children. They placed it in a shoe box nestled in soft grass clippings and Laurie took it to work. A hot line was established to a laboratory that raised baby bunnies and the formula for baby bunny milk was created. All week, doctors and nurses lined up during lunch hour to take their turn at bottle feeding baby bunny. Her eyes opened, her ears sprang up, and she was taken outside to explore the grass. And then one night, when she was being carried upstairs in her shoe box ~ she jumped out and broke her neck.

And the look in Heidi's eyes the morning after her mother Gretel died. Heidi sat alone and upright in my blue armchair recliner, a thing she had never done before (meaning she had never jumped up there by herself, without me lifting her). Waiting to catch my eye, waiting for me to acknowledge; *It's you and me, mum. It's us together.* She was so beautiful, so poignant, so vulnerable.

And her delight, her boundless enthusiasm ten days later with the arrival of seven-year-old Tiggy, a smaller longhaired Dachshund freshly released from life as a kennel dog, from life as brood bitch. What fun they had. Especially when it was time to go outside once more before bedtime; *YOU be the leader! I don't want to be the leader. Neither do I* ~ and they would turn as one and race down the corridor to bed. My bed (*our bed!*), and I would hurry after them, scoop them both up and try again; *YOU go first! I don't want to go first. Neither do I!* And off they would race again, ears flapping, tails flying. Eventually, being younger and faster, Tiggy won, and Heidi became the new pack leader. Up until now, she had done everything Gretel, her mother had ordained.

And the time Heidi carried a young groundhog half a mile to share with her friends. Nobody could believe she would do such a thing. Doors slammed, phones rang, all were convinced her victim must be rabid in order for her to have caught it. And the rats! They were building nests in the glove compartment of my car! I bought two traps, not that I could envision ever actually using them, but they were supposed to show the rats the seriousness of my intent, and I gave them fair warning they must leave or something dreadful would happen to them. They ignored me. Next day, I found two huge rats lying dead on the grass, and Heidi nearby, glancing meaningfully between them and me and looking very pleased and proud of herself!

And the time she got stuck under an old barn. Silence. Not a sound. Had a snake killed her? Did a groundhog have her in its death grip? Was her head stuck in a hole? Distraught, I ran to the big old house and came back with the owner, a no-nonsense elderly Brit in boots. She stomped violently on the barn floor and roared; GET OUT OF THERE HEIDI! And Heidi shot into the open air like a speeding arrow ~ covered in cobwebs and mouse droppings. Laughing!

And on a more nostalgic note, there was the time Heidi and Tiggy had their teeth cleaned. This involved anesthetic, and although Tiggy came home in good shape Heidi had remained under the influence much longer, while the veterinarian dug around for some roots of a rotten tooth. Twelve hours later she was still mostly unconscious. She trembled all over. I laid her in her softest bed and wrapped her in a goose down jacket. Tiggy was much concerned and lay beside her, and Heidi seemed to gain comfort by resting the tip of her nose against her little companion.

An hour later, she was still immobile and trembling, so I scooped her up and just held her tightly, still wrapped in a warm jacket. We sat in the recliner for another couple of hours. I never felt that she had actually left her body, I felt she was always there, but didn't have to stay in it if she didn't want to. I knew she could just float on out and not return if she wanted to. I told her that was alright, if that was what she wanted to do, but how happy Tiggy and I would be if she decided to stay. I told her I would support her if she chose to leave. I told her I would do everything to help her if she would stay. Unceasingly, I told her I loved her forever and always whatever she decided.

After nearly two hours, she stopped trembling, and although she never moved a muscle or twitched an eyelid, I knew the decision was made, and that she had shifted from being 'unconscious' to a deep, deep and peaceful sleep. I knew she had fully returned to her body; a change had taken place. At a deep inner level, there was a major energy shift as she slipped from a level of fathomless oblivion to deep, deep sleep. A couple of hours later I carried her outside which made her shake and tremble again, so we all went to bed, and snuggled down under the bedclothes. She eventually stopped trembling and after two or three days she was her usual wonderful self.

> "Jesus loved Lazarus and sent
> a powerful stream of Love towards him.
> This Love of Christ awakened and transformed
> the consciousness of Lazarus.
> Love awakened inside Lazarus,
> which awakened him physically as well.
> A change happened within the consciousness of Lazarus,
> and then the body came to life."
> ~ Peter Deunov (Beinso Douno)

I have asked Heidi for a Statement of Purpose, to speak what was on her heart;

Upon my heart is Love. Within my soul is Love, and it finds ways to Be ~ through me. In joy does it express the very core, the very essence of itself through ways I AM. In Love I live, and through this Love do I experience all things. Tiggy I love, and all who come, and it (the recent experience) was within the context of my Lov felt as a dimming and blurring of conscious memory and effect. That is why it helped so much when you held me, the love I felt from you was strong, empowering, merged with my own at all levels of my existence, my very molecules were touched. When I was alone, my Source seemed far away, the focus dimmed and blurred. And now? Life is eternal, you and I shall live forever. This is my thought, my heartsong for this day.

And the day after, as I was sitting cross-legged in the recliner, I asked that anything I needed to know be brought to my attention. I opened my eyes and saw that Heidi had come to sit in front of me. This was most unusual. Tiggy yes, but Heidi usually stays where she is. I pulled her up onto my lap, noting that Heidi comes to the music tape Majesty, whereas Tiggy comes to the Angelic music! Did Heidi have more to say?

Not Heidi so much as the lineage, the line of Power that she represents. She is of Dogdom, yes, but with a difference. For Heidi has transcended the world of dog. Not that this is in any way detrimental or superior to those of and in the Dog Kingdom, each have their own divine purpose and personal growth pattern to attend and manifest. But Heidi, like Jonathan Livingstone Seagull is one apart. One of those who have seen The Dream and has already risen in her mind ~ has made her Ascension. Truly. You feel it. Serenity and acceptance are words insufficient, inadequate for her current status, but they are worldly words with which we must make do. And Tiggy also knows this new Heidi. Recognizes and trusts with all her heart and being the divinity that is extended to her through this vehicle that she, that you and she love so well.

It crossed my mind to wonder at the purpose of this information.

Heidi is a Way Shower. What one can do by all may now be done. And each that follows, shall clarify and widen, make ever more accessible the open door for all to hear The Call, that each shall answer when they may. And as you have come to know, Heidi's time upon this plane is hers to choose, to do with as she wills. Her task complete, hers is the gift of Love, and truly does she now live in this (higher) dimension. Giving and receiving that which she is. She has no need to experience other than gentleness and love.

I had known without question that it was only love that brought Heidi back to stay with us. I knew that if she had stayed overnight at the veterinary clinic, she would not be with us now. It was a miracle in itself that they had allowed a mostly unconscious dog to go home! And I noticed how the experience had drawn Tiggy and Heidi even closer together, to such an extent that others remarked upon it. Certainly it seemed that the 'unconscious' experience had allowed more of her soul essence in, she had received an upgrade.

And then, I was contemplating the phrase from A Course in Miracles, 'Let not my mind deny the thought of God.' I was sitting on my little seat amongst the pine trees, when Heidi unexpectedly appeared beside me. Tiggy liked to come and sit on the bit of sheepskin in front of me, but Heidi usually kept her distance. I hauled her aboard anyway, onto my lap. Is Heidi a thought of God?

Yes! Heidi is a thought of God. She is giving you an opportunity to express your love. To express your higher qualities, your higher Self. 'God is but Love' applies to both of you. Dogs, especially your dogs, express this most beautifully.

Perhaps I think of her because we are nearing the first anniversary of her Ascension, and because Jamala continues with his reports of Heidi, Tiggy and Loreli visiting him in his morning meditations. And as so often, my mind is drawn to wonder, what exactly did Heidi do?! And how?! Immediately. Clearly. Telepathically, words come;

Heidi did what Heidi came to do. Heidi spun her molecules at such a vibratory pitch, such a mathematical frequency of finesse, that they accelerated her bodily parts into a higher dimension, involving her in the phenomena known as invisibility. Heidi's presence is still available if the requirement of her presence were necessary. But it was not her purpose to remain in dog form in the ethers. It is possible, but it was not deemed necessary by Heidi. The angel that Jamala sees is a game she plays, a beautiful game. A game of the heart. And it is his heart flame that keeps the embers glowing, so to speak. As Gretel played with you (for three years Gretel taught me higher truths in my meditations), so does Heidi play with Jamala. And when we say play, it is not as children play with their toys, it is the Game of Life. It is the Game of Eternity stepped down in frequency to allow participation by one in physical form, by one in human form. For there is great purpose in this Game. They are the featured performers, the featured players, she and Jamala, in this enactment of a play that caters to the needs of others, that serves as a backdrop for others to play their part. Back to your question. What is the difference, you ask, between what Heidi did and what you shall do?

For some time now, I have envisioned myself doing a 'modified Heidi'. Modified in that I shall return, come and go, in and out of form, rather than withdraw altogether.

You too will learn to do as Heidi did. Vibrate your molecules at such a frequency that you will appear invisible and find yourself in a higher frequency dimension. But unlike Heidi, you shall maintain the pattern of your physical form handy. Handy we shall say that you may lower yourself into it whenever the need arises. You will be able to do this at will, speeding up and slowing down the vibratory rate, the frequency exchange of your molecules. And so, you will maintain a physical abode for appearances sake, for the purpose of the job in hand. And into this abode, you will learn to lower that which is needed to maintain this facade, out of the atmosphere, out of the ethers. As you lower your own body into form, so will you be able to lower (in frequency) what you need, what is needed to maintain your lifestyle. When will this be? It will not be abruptly nor all at once. It will be in bits and pieces. It will be an easing into this new frequency or lifestyle. But it will seem to you oh so natural ~ a very natural occurrence. You are practicing it now, are you not? You are perfecting the art now of drawing from the ethers what you want and need to complete your mission. The Law of Attraction, the art of manifestation.

And what will be the purpose, you wonder? Of raising your particles into the ethers, if you must return. It will be by choice. It will be as regeneration; it will be as spiritual food. As now you choose to be alone, as now you have special preferences, so then will that be your special preference. And you will gather with others doing similar work, for when we say 'you', we include all 'yous'. And you will meet with the Masters as you call them, your co-workers who remained in spirit as we see them. And when you leave for the final time ~ there will not be a final time, and until that time, Sananda (my home) is your pivotal point, your focus of power, your strength of purpose.

Every part and particle, every molecule, every atom and subatomic electron of Heidi's being accelerated at a vibratory spin so fast that they became pure energy. This is the warmth that she experienced, and that you experienced. And as they continued to spin ever faster, at a frequency you cannot imagine, this was the expansion. This was the expansion into the beyond ~ and beyond and beyond. They spun faster than the speed of light. They passed through light and expanded beyond all boundaries into the infinite beyond.

Heidi did not ascend to fifth or sixth dimensions, not even seventh. Heidi expanded, fast forwarded herself into infinity. This is not your purpose at this time. Your purpose is to halt, to stop. To accelerate only so far. To go higher or to spin faster at this time, makes it very difficult to also maintain contact in a tangible form within physical existence. But from the fifth and sixth dimensions you may come and go as your bodily parts accelerate, your understanding grows, and the veil becomes thinner. ~ We are the Brotherhood of Light, with blessings and thanks to those in Service on planet Earth. God bless.

This was news to me! About the fifth, sixth and seventh dimensions! I could only trust that I was hearing, receiving and reporting correctly. I also received the feeling or knowing, that the higher the frequency or dimension attained, the greater the energy that would be required to lower oneself into form. Years passed before I read of others sharing similar thoughts and information, and was so excited to read the following that I promptly contacted Sal, who then came to visit a few times.

"When you reach 5th density, you are no longer on the wheel of incarnation and are now on the Ascension spiral. Those in the higher densities do not easily materialize a physical form and walk upon the Earth. Almost never done. Very difficult, and the chance of getting caught in the lower densities if we did materialize directly into them, is why we come through channels, telepathically, radiating our energy into your aura, diluted." ~ *Sal Rachele*

Also, by this time, I was receiving transmissions from other people's animals explaining exactly this, that if they went higher than the 5th or 6th dimensions, it would be very difficult for them to return to earth as their human loved ones so desired. They also specifically indicated that this, returning to earth, could also cause the risk of being caught up in the wheel of life ~ the revolving doorway!

January 1995 ~ The Merkabah

The thought has come to wonder what Tiggy and Loreli experienced that magical night. I ask Tiggy for her perception of Heidi's Ascension. You were all asleep Tiggy, it was late at night when Heidi woke you. Usually you didn't want to go out that late, did you? Can you tell me what you thought, what you felt, what you saw? Tiggy was sleeping, but she agreed to talk anyway. In my mind, she said;

We felt excitement. We felt Heidi's excitement, me and Loreli. We knew something was happening. We didn't know what. We didn't know Heidi was going to be the happening. We knew Heidi knew something exciting was going on, and we followed her. We were all set to follow her lead. But she vanished! We didn't see which way she went, where she went. We all ran out together, and Heidi left us. And there were no bunnies out there. We thought Heidi was going to lead us on a bunny hunt, but no ~ there was nothing out there, so we came back inside.

"When Jesus had thus said, he disappeared,
and no one saw him go.
His disciples did not comprehend the change,
they knew not where their master went,
and they went on their way."
~ The Aquarian Gospel of Jesus the Christ

Oh! Now I have more questions! Does that mean Heidi was becoming invisible before she got to the place where the footprints stopped? *Yes,* came the answer in my head. *As Cinderella must leave the ball before midnight, so Heidi began to dissolve before she had reached her position ~ dissolved to the physical eyes that is. Her form, her solid form was still apparent, for it made footprints did it not?*

And I wondered about the beam of light around Heidi. How did it get there? What was its function? Who put it there?

Nobody put it there, dear one, she magnetized it. She magnetized it to herself by the vibratory rate of her molecular spin. She attracted this photonic beam to act as an insulator, an encapsulation against outside disturbances or distractions. It ensured that nothing would occur to interfere or deter the intent of her focus to ascend. To return from whence she came.

With this photon beam around her, no passing owl may snatch her in its claws, nor wayward ship abduct, for she was defenseless once the process had begun. Her bodily parts became immobilized, and she would be unable to run or defend herself in any manner should outside interference occur.

This beam created a safe haven for her to do her thing, you might say, and is, we might add, ecofriendly and biodegradable. No remnant shall be left or found; it shall simply return its elements to the source of its origin. It has an intelligence of its own. Indeed, the Merkabah you may term it, an ascension vehicle or chamber.

And it would stay around her as long as needed, as long as her frequency held it in place, would it be with her. But you would not have seen it taking off toward the heavens like a skyrocket, or one of your fourth of July fireworks, had you been observing. Oh, no. For Heidi was absorbed back into the infinity of the Universe where she stood. She did not go anywhere, she was simply breathed back into the infinite, into Infinity. And as a point of consciousness she could locate, could bilocate in any manner place or form in which she wished. And her function at this time, her purpose at this time, is with the Violet Flame, the Flame of Freedom, the Sacred Flame of Transformation. Amongst the Archangelic Host of this Flame, she Serves in Love.

Once more, I ask the dogs if they have anything to add. Tiggy sleeps on, but in my mind, Loreli's eyes, alert and bright, watch me intently;

We wondered, we wondered greatly why you kept getting up all night to look for her. It was a puzzlement to us why you did this. For we knew that you knew she would not return. And yes, it was difficult for us to adjust to living without her physical presence. She told us what to do, and how to do it. And even though we didn't always do exactly as she told us, it was a great comfort and security to have her there. She was a place for us to come home to. And when we slept ~ she would take us with her sometimes, on her journeys. I loved that. I loved that when she took me journeying in my sleep. We went to very exciting places and she showed us things. She wouldn't let us go into the places that she showed us, she said we wouldn't be able to come back if we did.

Regarding the danger of entering a Higher Frequency in consciousness unprepared;

"Let us protect ourselves with the Ring Pass Not of Cosmic Christ Lightening, as well as sustain around us our Cloak of Invisibility to protect us from lower frequencies that might impede our Ascension Process. Here, Beloved Lord Michael and his Legions assist in keeping us focused and protected. Here we stand in Lord Michael's Circle and Sword of Blue Flame, the Sword being our Rod of Power and Protection, and the Circle of Blue Flame being our Sphere of Influence, inclusive of all life living free in the Light. We see the base upon which we stand as the Sun of Elemental Constancy out of which streams a Mighty Blue Lightening Ray of Cosmic Christ Protection from anything less than the

Divine Potential. We stand enveloped in this Cosmic Ray, now safe to explore 'beyond time and space'". ~ *abbreviated from Ascended and Free*

I asked Loreli if she and Tiggy still went to these places, without Heidi. *Well, not really. It's better to have a guide in those places.* What did she show you? Where did she take you? *It's difficult to describe. It's like when you wake up, you forget your dream. But it was very exciting. Very wondrous. Very amazing to know all these things exist. She doesn't communicate with us directly, but she lets us know that all is well with her, and she encourages us. She encourages us in the things we do. And she says she loves us, and we know she does. She says I have my own guides who work with me.*

And I recalled a meditation three weeks before Heidi left. It was New Year's Day, 1994, and I had asked if Heidi had guides who work with her. Words came;

Indeed she does. Angel ones. Great Beings of Light. Angelic Beings who work with her and hold the forcefield, the energy of their realm, the realm from whence she came ~ around her.

And I recalled another time when we were sitting out between the Pines, Heidi, Tiggy, Loreli and me, and I asked if the dogs had anything to say.

We love the feel of the sun on our bodies. And the song of the birds enters our dream as we lie on the earth and travel on distant journeys. Where do you go? *Heidi travels within the deeper realms. Heidi can travel to the depth of her consciousness. And Tiggy is exploring in child-like manner with her freshly sprouted wings, (this is how I saw her! With dear little new wings), and as they mature and grow in strength, she too will fly higher, go deeper, travel further and stay in these realms longer. At present she must keep coming back, returning for air so to speak, for another breath before continuing the wonderment of her new explorations.* Do they meet with Gretel? *Occasionally Gretel and Heidi meet and merge and travel deep together.*

"Animals are multidimensional and in sleep state visit other worlds. So do people, but they don't know that, and animals do." ~ *Matthew*

January 1995 ~ The Dimensional Doorway

It is just over a year since Heidi left us, and a friend has asked me to define the 11.11, 12.12, 3.33, 4.44, and 5.55. Dimensional doorways, I replied glibly. It satisfied us both at the time and we passed to other things. Thinking upon this later, I understand that in her leaving, Heidi opened a dimensional doorway. I ask for more information on this. Is this dimensional doorway just in that vicinity, or is it the whole garden of Sananda?

She did indeed open the doorway. Not create it, for it was in existence, it was in effect, but it was Heidi's passage through that opened it up, so to speak. And the entire sanctuary is a vortex, a dimensional portal in which there are different openings into different frequencies. The one in the center of your room (a large carpeted living room where we have many gatherings), you know as the portal to the center of the Earth, of which you are the gate keeper. And Heidi's portal would be as one that goes straight, direct to the higher realms. And the one over the crystal (in the garden), that has been referred to as the Ascension Chamber would be seen more as an atomic accelerator.

And each time these vortex or portals are utilized, they are more firmly established, more firmly anchored, more firmly developed. As constant use of solid matter creates wear and tear, so does frequent creative play in these areas allow a thinning of the ethers around them. They may be seen as eddies, or whirlpools of energy that are strengthened as the energies converge and grow stronger each time they are used or utilized.

And so, you may think of this vortex as an eddy or whirlpool of energy that was developing, and into which Heidi was drawn. And by her use was a particular frequency established. She did not create it, but she birthed it into your realm we may say. The one in the center of your room has developed through constant use. Heidi's was created or brought into effect by the combined energies of the pines, the crystal and the water beneath the well, they drew the energies unto themselves, creating this highly energized vortex.

And the entire sanctuary of Sananda is a vortex in that it pulsates at a higher frequency or vibration than the surrounding territory. It may draw to itself, it has magnetized great Beings of Light who work, or network their energies through the radiance of this place. Thus may it be termed a portal ~ a portal for those of the higher realms to work through, into the denser vibrations that surround.

And although nothing is impossible, and it would not be a waste of their energies to work directly, it would be as an ineffectual use of power. To work through such a place as this magnifies and radiates their frequencies more efficiently, in a more organized manner. Much as you distribute your worldly goods to refugees of great disasters through an organization ~ so do these great Ones of Light find it convenient to work through Sananda. Understand, it is the etheric counterpart of which we speak.

January 1995 ~ The Call to Ascension

I am remembering the electrified sense of expectancy I experienced before Heidi's departure. For months I was on a high with joy. No matter what seemed out of alignment or didn't work, I remained euphoric. Heidi too was unreasonably joyful! Especially for an elder dog! Was it that at some level of my being I recognized the energies, something in the air, the ethers, that bore a resemblance, that related to an Ascension I had known in another time, another place? I have asked for insight and clarification on this.

Yes, dear one, it was a recognition. Not on a cellular level, nor yet within your DNA, but within the very patterning, the geometric formula or structure of your essence. Within the pulsations of your wave form was this frequency recognized. A very subtle energy that preceded an event of monumental proportions. For the very ethers reflected or bore the knowingness that lay within this one for whom Ascension called.

> *For Ascension is a word only that denotes a call,*
> *a tone, a song, a beckoning from an unformed hand*
> *to a song unsung, a tune unplayed.*
> *This call to Ascension lies formless in the void,*
> *a sound unheard that stirs*
> *and sings unto itself a note*
> *too long away from its symphonic home.*

And it was this unsung song, this vibratory pulse that resonated with your own, and glimmered in your heart, a long-forgotten rhythm that brought great joy, from depths untold to conscious mind. And you shall know this tune again. Next time it plays, it plays for you, and you shall dance as Heidi danced, and know a sweetness through your cells that brings release, a rebirth into Freedom. As when a single note from one small bird sings winter into spring, so shall the celebration of your emergence to the Sun be heralded by this Wave of Sound you call Ascension.

And these returning waves shall gently lap the shoreline of that distant realm, and as they roll, so shall they gain in force. And as the pressure builds, they shall roll faster ~ vaster, greater and more frequently they come.

And Sound shall build in Silence,
as each and every standing wave returneth home.
Merging in oneness to create an ocean of each other,
an ocean of one Self.
An ocean that shall know each droplets lifetime as its own,
and wash away the tears and share the joy.
And rolling in upon itself
this ocean shall rise up once more,
greet the New Day and standing
by the Angel of the Cosmic Dawn proclaim
I AM, I AM, I AM THAT I AM.

"Heidi was the perfect wave!" ~ Dan Winter (smiling!)

New Moon January 1995 ~ Heidi's Love

This seems as good a place as any to pause. There is no end. Heidi lives on, her essence is eternal. Her work with Jamala continues, and some have seen her dancing in the garden in her Heidi-dog form. Dancing on her hind legs and laughing. Eyes shining, ears flapping, and laughing. She comes when we have happy gatherings of friends she knew. Holographic images she sends to bring us joy. To make us smile. To brighten our day and lighten our hearts. To quicken our frequency, to accelerate our understanding and consciousness.

And then one day, as I was contemplating the new Cosmic frequencies said to be emanating from the 5th dimensional crystalline solar Violet Flame and descending to Earth at this time, I thought of Heidi and heard;

Dearest One, Heidi herself is a Cosmic Being, as are all your dogs ~ or emanations of those who wished to add their frequency to your garden, the Garden of Sananda. What better way to do this? Most convenient, from our point of view! They would receive the Love they needed to maintain existence in form and be ever surrounded by Peace and Beauty. And what fun they had! For even they did not know what their creations would become! Free will, in as much as they must release these creations (the dogs), to comply with the laws of 3rd dimensional existence, where, we hesitate to say ~ they lost control! For their creations, in this case the dogs, were free to act in accordance with their design or matrix (the format of dog). And we repeat, what fun they had! Who are we? Who do you think we are!

I supposed they were those who came as or were responsible for those who came as the ten little dachshunds. And I heard *'right on'*!

She Walked Away

I continue to think often of Heidi. Her demonstration. And a profound phrase that has been coming to me recently regarding change and how we adjust to it ~ *you walk away*. Re-listening to an old audio tape that was channeled for me seemingly eons ago, I heard;

And you walked into the desert, and you ascended.

And I had a clear and beautiful vision of many people, just walking forward, and randomly disappearing into another dimension. And I thought of Heidi ~ *she walked away!* She walked away from everything she loved! She walked away from Tiggy and Loreli whom she loved so very much. She walked away from her warm cozy bed and her furry blanket; she walked away from *me*! And I shed a tear. But she didn't walk ~ *she ran!!!* Barking joyfully!

The End

There is no End

Beloved Heidi
"Gone, Gone, Gone Beyond.
Gone, Altogether Beyond.
Oh, what an Awakening! All Hail!"
~ *from the Heart Sutra of the Buddha*

The Ascension of Gretel

September 1987

Gretel was Heidi's mother. A kennel dog for the first five years of her life. Gretel loved everyone, and everyone loved Gretel. Nothing fazed her. Most dogs are afraid of the vacuum cleaner. Not Gretel. She would lie stretched out on the carpet and if the vacuum gently ruffled her fur, she would happily flutter her abundantly furry tail ~ *I love you too vacuum cleaner!* Same with cars, she would stand in the driveway gently wagging her tail at the oncoming vehicle and as the drivers frantically honked their horns, Gretel would silently beam ~ *I love you too cars!* One day we took six little dogs on a field trip around a lake. Pretty soon Gretel went missing. Turning back, I was dismayed to see her swimming far out across the water to visit with a flock of geese! Ignoring my shrieks and pleas, she swam happily on and around them, seemingly just to say ~ *I love you too Geese* and headed back to shore. At other times she took herself for little swims in the river. All of which gave me extreme anxiety! Especially the time a big fierce German Shepherd charged forward to gobble her all up, only to halt abruptly as Gretel stood undeterred with gently wagging tail beaming ~ I love you too big dog. My shattered companions informed me that he had killed two little dogs the previous week. And I heard within my mind the words;

It was not fearlessness that Gretel expressed, for fearlessness itself can have an aggravating rub. It was the quality of harmlessness that she emanates so purely and so well.

"Harmlessness ~ when we are at peace with ourselves, we emanate a living, peaceful energy that others respond to, whether consciously aware of it or not. They sense somehow that we are not a threat, that we are kind and gentle." ~ *Bob and Judy Carpenter*

Ever loving and caring, Gretel and Heidi pioneered bringing comfort and joy to the elderly in nursing homes. Once, after gently kissing the fragile fingers of a small and withered hand, we heard a small voice whisper, "Oh, Gretel! You just made my day!" The nurses said this little lady hadn't spoken all week. And Gretel saved the lives of other dogs.

We were living on a large estate taking care of the horses. It was early morning and I had just opened the gate and called them in for their morning feed when I heard Gretel barking. It was no ordinary bark, it had an urgent, sharp and hollow ring. Turning, I saw across the paddock, passed the chicken house (a wonder in itself as Gretel loved to sit and watch the chickens), and over the driveway, Gretel was racing up the hill towards the main house and the swimming pool, with Heidi galloping after her ~ and me now hurrying after both of them. Breathless, I arrived to find Gretel standing at the edge of the pool, continuing to give the alarm as two young lurcher puppies floundered around in the water. About the size of a small greyhound, they were less than a year old and couldn't find the way out. The owners were away but Gretel's relentless commotion brought a somewhat sleepy and befuddled pet sitter to the scene and between the two of us we dragged the sodden pups from the water. How did Gretel know what was happening? She was a considerable distance away, with no physical means of seeing or hearing what was happening ~ and the pool itself was surrounded by huge boxwoods.

Gretel was a happy, healthy, loving and much-loved little dog. And so it was with much surprise that one day when she was 13 years old, I found myself looking at her in a dream like state and thinking, *I wonder how Gretel will die?* This was a very strange thought. Why would I think such a thing? As the day wore on, I supposed I had better do something about this strange thought. In those days, I was not comfortable with the words 'God' or 'prayer', so I called it a request. I asked that when her time came, she would go in gentleness and peace, in her own bed, in her own home, with soft music playing and her friends around her. Strangely, I added that it didn't matter if I was there or not, as long as friends she loved were around her.

Two years later, this is *exactly* what happened. Gretel woke up coughing and I knew 'this was the day'. I had a prior obligation, so I left soft music playing and arranged for friends to visit her, to sit beside and just be with her. I took Heidi to spend the day with another friend. By the time I got home Gretel had left her body. Next morning, our friend the plumber 'just happened' to arrive early for our small meditation group. Plumbers have digging tools. He was also Gretel's very good friend and gently buried her body beneath the pines.

Healthy to the end, Gretel left me on a high with joy for her safe transition. For the next three days I was almost delirious with joy! If anyone had asked me how Gretel was, they would have thought I had lost my mind. She *died!* Woohoo! It was years before I realized it was *her* joy I was feeling. Many years later still, I understood it was *my own joy* that I was experiencing. That my love for Gretel *entrained* me to her joy.

This interdimensionality will become so commonplace in your development of Mastery that, come your final 'passing' permanently into the next Realm of formlessness, you will do so at the exact moment you choose, when it is perfect for your life and your service to Earth. You will do so in a Forcefield of complete Peace, Victory, Completion, Graduation and Ascension ~ as is done on all other Perfected Planets. And those around you will be left only with Happiness and Gratitude at your personal Victory, for they will know only a deeper Communion of Spirit with you than ever they did when you were in a body. ~ Group Avatar

I could hardly wait to meditate, to send Gretel my love! But I had read about earth-bound spirits, anchored to the physical realms through their loved one's grief or clinging thoughts, and I had no desire to bind Gretel to my wishes. So I was cautious, I started and ended every exchange by saying, I love you Gretel, and she always replied ~ *I love you too.*

The next morning I played soft music, I told Gretel how much I loved her, how much I wanted the very best for her, that she must look for the Light and follow her bliss. I began by imagining her in a beautiful place I knew she would like. I saw her snuffling around a gentle stream that extended into a large shallow pond. There was green grass and flowers, and rocks and insects, and birds and clouds, all the things that Gretel loved. After a little while, because I didn't want her to get lonely ~ I had a big dog come by and help her look for things. Gretel loved big dogs. And then I realized evening was drawing nigh, and I didn't want Gretel to be all by herself, so between us, we saw a little cottage we hadn't noticed before, and in the cottage was a little old lady who welcomed Gretel and explained that she was waiting for her own little dog who was still on Earth, and she invited Gretel to stay as long as she would like. And so I left them together. By this time I wasn't sure what I had imagined and what was real.

And so, for the next three years, Gretel became my spiritual mentor, my master teacher. Gently, in my meditations, she taught me about mindfulness, how to listen, to sense, to be aware. She taught me about multi-dimensional living, universal truths, the true meaning of unconditional Love, and how to 'die' in Love. She taught me to commune with Nature and the Great I AM. She taught me via her own spiritual expansion, presenting herself as the Golden Gretel, or in what I called her Radiant, or her 'see-through', and 'glass' bodies.

"Once matter has been impregnated by Spirit, it will become transparent. Even the trees, even the rocks, even man's physical body, everything will become crystalline and radiant." ~ *Omraam Mikhael Aïvanhov*

At that time, I had never heard of the Body of Light, the Crystal Body, the Diamond Body, or The Body of Glory. She allowed me to discover for myself that she was an emanation of my own twin Angel, come to bring me comfort and joy. And every time she led me into a greater awareness, a higher perspective, an expanded understanding, I thought *that was it!* My mind simply could not conceive of anything new to experience after each revelation! And then we would start the next spiral of my spiritual unfoldment.

At that time in my life, I would go to a beautiful temple I had created in my mind for my meditations, and so, a week later, I invited Gretel to join me there. And she came! My beloved Gretel came! Looking just as I had last seen her, only more beautiful, her coat more vibrant, her eyes more brilliant, her whole self more alert and joyful. I told her how much I loved her ~ but that she was free to do whatever she needed to do. The next day, she came again, and she looked *magnificent!* It was Gretel, but it was a *glorious* Gretel. On the third day, she was moving towards me, her eyes scrunched tight with concentration, trying to ~ trying to, I couldn't imagine what she was trying to do. And suddenly ~ she was flying! Swimming through the air like an otter in water. Diving, circling, spiraling, laughing ~ and I was laughing too. I put out my arms to her and she dived between them, swooshing past me and twisting out of reach. *Laughing*. I called it flying ~ my friends said she was showing me that she was *free*.

Because of this, I didn't check in with Gretel for a while, and then one day when I was asking to be taught something in my meditations, suddenly, there was Gretel, struggling upward through the void, striving to go somewhere. Her concentration was intense, and it bothered me that I couldn't see whether her eyes were open or shut. I was devastated. This wasn't my Gretel; this wasn't my own darling Gretel anymore. This was a little dog with a purpose and goal of its own. Tears rolled down my cheeks. I was an observer only. *What is she doing?* And immediately I saw the Golden Gretel, a great and glorious, poised and laughing Golden Gretel filled my vision. She directed her joy and love to the still toiling small Gretel, whose intent and purpose seemed ever more intense as it drew near. I felt the longing within this little dog to just get home and rest for ever more, and finally ~ the drab and weary little Gretel disappeared inside the glorious Golden Gretel who turned away and dissolved into Light.

What did this mean? Immediately words came to mind ~ *your higher selves are always up there rooting for you.*

And so the weeks went by, and I did not look for Gretel. I thought *that was it!* But I thought of her often and was told she was 'learning things'. That she was 'learning very much in the vehicle of the canine consciousness and would be around the earth plane for two or three years, available for me if I wished to maintain the contact'. I couldn't imagine what the implications of *not* being available to me could possibly mean!

And then one day, I just *had* to know what Gretel was doing! What *could* she be learning? I started to visualize her ~ and she appeared! Happy and beautiful, but she was down below me, barking up at me, *wow, wow, wow!* Waggy, waggy tail. Very happy, very excited. I was appalled! What had I done, that she was below me! In my mind I had to lean over and look down at her; Gretel, what *are* you doing down there? You don't have to be below me. Come on up here with me! *Wow, wow, wow!* What's happened? Can you still fly? *Oh yes, I can still fly if I want to.* She acted like that was no big deal. Well, what happened to the Golden Gretel? *I only went there for a quick rest. Now, off to work!* Gretel! Can you tell me what you're doing? No response. In fact, Gretel seemed to be getting rather bored and was beginning to fade. "Of course," said a friend, "she was impatient with you for not understanding she was being a *dog!*"

Well Gretel, if you can't *tell* me what you're doing, can you *show* me? Immediately I was overcome with the sensation of a multitude of dogs and cats. *Really?!* Cats too?! And I was given the feeling, the awareness, that Gretel was teaching the dogs about love, about loving the cats. Was this for real?! And a nondescript sandy colored cat wrapped itself around Gretel, tail in air, tip kinked over. *Gretel is teaching them to love their neighbor.* It seemed that Gretel had returned to a lower level of consciousness, a denser vibration, to do this ~ and at that moment I was in a higher one, giving me the illusion of looking down on her.

Weeks passed, and I decided to check up on the cat therapy program. Whenever I thought of her nowadays, my mind was filled with an image of the joyful, laughing Golden Gretel. I expressed my love for her and invited her to speak.

I love you too. My work continues. The cats are responsive because my helpers are like myself, and the cats trust us. Even the fearful cats that had bad experiences with dogs, they learn from watching the other cats. So these pioneer cats will be teachers too. And when we have enough teachers and are confident, and the time is ripe, we will all go forth to teach the masses, the multitudes of ignorant dogs and cats, to love one another. In these realms and on earth.

Does this mean that you will take physical form again? *I may. I may. As the call comes, here I AM. I love you Gretel. I know. I know. I love you too.*

Meanwhile, Gretel continued to be a regular visitor in my Temple, the Temple I had created in my mind and which took on a life of its own. Other regular visitors were various Ascended Masters, fairies, assorted nature spirits, birds, and the other dogs. It seemed to be a time of learning, fun and play for all. Gretel was on familiar terms with everyone. Sometimes she would trot in behind the Masters, sometimes they would follow her out! The fairies loved to ride on her long back and slide down her tail!

On one occasion, when Gretel was already waiting there to greet us ~ me, Tiggy, Loreli and whoever, she was in what I called her Radiant Body and very pleased to see us. Did she get lonely when we didn't come I worried? Where was she all the time? What are you doing Gretel?

I await the unfoldment of my plan. Eventually a door will open, a light will shine, a way will be shown, a path will reveal itself, and I shall choose to follow it or I shall return to the Light. And I must keep myself on the alert. Ever ready. Ever prepared to offer my Services. To Serve the Cause to which I have pledged my existence. This is my place to wait.

Oh, that's beautiful, Gretel. I am so privileged to know you. I am so privileged to have you as my friend. I really felt this ~ this feeling that I am in the Presence of a much higher being than myself. Angel Gretel! May I call you angel Gretel? *You may call me Angel Gretel*, she turned away with a smile. I can't say how she did this, but I had the feeling of when one turns away to hide a smile from a small child who just said something innocent and adorable. And I thought, you must have a higher name! An angelic name? She turned away again, smiling, *I do!* And I heard the name, *Glorianandama*. And I feel a great motherly love emanating from Gretel for she is one of Mary's Holy Angels and I heard, *that is why you thought of her as 'mother of the world', 'mother of all things'. That was the quality she expressed for Mary.*

> "Regarding Angels ~ this energy is also
> quite capable of interacting with you
> in the form of a 'Totem' or through a household pet."
> ~ *Archangel Metatron, through James Tyberonn*

On another occasion, my Temple was a very beautiful nature setting, with a little waterfall and a sparkling clear pool trickling away in a merry little stream, and soft green grass. Gretel you would love it here! And there she is! So beautiful. Gretel you are so beautiful! Her coat is magnificent, she is in her Gretel-dog body, but so beautiful, and she is very happy. But I have to step down, climb down to Gretel and my Temple.

Why is this? She is very pleased to see me, to know that I know where she is.

Your beloved Gretel is working again. Not in the lower astral levels as she did before. Then she was with cat chasers, cat killers. 'Bad dogs'! But she is lower none the less than you are accustomed to going in your meditations. She is working with those in transition. Those who have been traumatized. Gently she will lead them to a place of love and beauty. A safe haven such as this. She would appear to them as a queen mother. And I had the feeling of Gretel as a Mother Mary of the dog world. The divine mother principle which they may trust unconditionally, these victims of loveless lives and anguished deaths. *Your Gretel will offer them, remind them of the only love they ever knew, fleeting moments of a mother's care. And they will allow Gretel to nurse them back to health, in mind and spirit. And as before, she will train others in her ways and rise once more on spirit wings between the stars. Meanwhile, she waits for you ~ she will not journey Home alone.*

I felt that she was also conscious of being on hand in case Heidi should need her. Early next morning I awoke to the words ~ *for Gretel knows only love. An angel among angels. And all are blessed who walk on Gretel's path. Glori Ananda Ma by name, and glorious mother of bliss by nature. She is God smiling to be sure! Gretel has been with you through the night. Treats for herself and blessings for you!*

The New Year came. I thought of Gretel and told her how much I loved her. For the first time there was no image of Gretel or her higher self. I decided to imagine her anyway. I would ask her if there was anything I could do to help her. Before I could do so, words flowed into my mind, gentle, but commanding;

You cannot help me in the spirit world, for you are in the physical. You can help on that level, by preparing the way for My return. I was overcome with emotion, totally overwhelmed by the feeling that this was more like the Christ speaking than Gretel ~ *preparing people in their minds. Helping them to experience love, to watch for loving acts.* The feeling that this was the Christ speaking grew ever stronger ~ *to notice loving gifts, not material ones, but gifts of loving concern. To start practicing loving thoughts, for themselves and others. And as they practice and become proficient, so will the awareness and love for*

God's other kingdoms grow. But they must start with that in hand. They must start by loving themselves. Gretel, you are speaking with such assurance and authority. *Oh yes, I too have grown. I too AM THAT I AM. I too can focus the Light and beam it far.*

My mind really couldn't cope with all this! Are you still working? Teaching the dogs to love the cats? *This work is passing to others. I come at times to advise, to encourage.* And then with great gentleness came the words, *I have returned to the Light.*

I saw and felt nothing but Light, and the sense that where or what Gretel was now, was totally incomprehensible to me at this present moment. My mind was blown. With great love and tenderness, as one would explain something to a child, she added, *I am no longer in my form as Gretel.*

Small wonder I had been unable to conjure up an image of her! My friends accepted this unconditionally. "Any questions we would have asked Gretel, we now ask the Christ," they said, "for Gretel has become the Christ." It certainly seemed as though Gretel was either speaking through the Christ, or the Christ was speaking through Gretel. She had merged or flowed into Oneness, Unity Consciousness. I asked for clarification on this and heard that Gretel now knew herself as an extension of the Light and that she had access to all knowledge. Obviously, I thought ~ *that was it!*

> "The Cosmic Christ speaks through countless voices
> within the collective goodness of Humanity,
> as well as the Angels and the Elementals,
> all aspects of the Great I AM expressing on Earth."
> ~ *Lord Maitrya, Ascended and Free*

However! My next experience with Gretel included a moment of panic when I not only couldn't conjure up an image of her, *I couldn't remember what she looked like.* I was so upset. What's the matter with me? Very softly, very gently, she breathed the thought into my mind;

> *There is no reason to remember what I looked like,*
> *for I have returned to the Light. I too AM That I AM.*

And my entire mind was again filled with a glory and brilliance so great, so totally unexpected and overwhelming, that I had no meaningful way of processing the experience, and simply opened my eyes and got on with my day as best I could. Shaken to the core!

A couple of months later I was meditating between the Pine trees, thinking of Gretel. Suddenly I was aware of her.

She comes because she too has treasured memories. Not because she needs to, but because it is enjoyable to re-experience one's memories on occasion. To savor each detail in full, relishing only the joy and love that was present. Re-creating it without the worldly ties and conditions that physical embodiment reconstitutes. She is with you in spirit only. She wants to share only spirit joy with you. Her Light essence. There is no need for either of you to contemplate the form she took, the house in which she dwelled, the vehicle for that embodiment. She comes to visit as a Being of Light, simply to share her glorious presence with one she loves dearly.

Once again, I was sitting outside between the Pines and asked for clarification, for insight, for enlightenment ~ what does all this Gretel stuff really mean?

It means that Gretel is within her angelic self. Her angelic being. It means that she has risen beyond the confines of earthly strictures and is truly oriented with her glorious Self. Because she has released, has worked through all earthly ties, she is free to fly with the angels. To be the Golden Angel that she truly is. And from this point she may operate as and where she wills.

The physical unit of Gretel, as we have said, is a very convenient vehicle for us to use, to further the Cause, the purpose of Divine Will made manifest upon and in all levels of existence. Thus do the Brotherhood take her with them, as one of them, doing the Work, the Service that she feels called to do. That is her calling, to re-unite the dogs, the canines, and the humans as one.

And she will be a part of the new Eden, the New Earth, greeting in love all who come to express, to give expression to the concept of heaven on earth. The Golden Gretel will be a focus for the blending, the merging of the shared hopes, inspired beliefs and integration of the life streams that shall come, that shall return to give their all to the glory of Creation's Truth.

I forget exactly what Gretel was up to in the following meditation or 'teaching', but it was something that made me wonder how she could possibly do such a thing! Be everywhere at once, in so many different locations helping so many all at the same time. And she gave me an image of her Golden, Glorious, or Angelic Self sending forth what looked like an endless stream or spray of little Gretels wherever they were needed. Gob smacked again, I hurried off to the friendly nun at the local Buddhist Temple to share my latest Gretel story. She stared at me in delighted amazement and announced, "Oh! She's a little Bodhisattva!" I wasn't quite sure exactly what that was, but Alana, who gave classes in Buddhism, looked at me in wonder and added, seemingly in awe, "that's a very advanced teaching!"

In Tibetan Buddhism, I learned a Bodhisattva is anyone who is motivated by compassion and seeks enlightenment not only for him or herself but also for everyone. Gretel apparently is such a one, ever returning to help others, until all are free from suffering.

~ ~ ~ ~ ~

I had been gathering Gretel's file together. Three years' worth. We had not been in touch for some time, but now, naturally she was on my mind as I sat for meditation. I told her how much I loved her and invited her to my Temple. Nothing. I envisioned my little Gretel. Nothing. The Golden Gretel ~ was dullish. The crystal Gretel, beautiful, but just an ornament. Gradually it dawned on me, the game was over. Words came;

We don't need to play the game anymore. We don't need to keep up the pretense. You know Who I AM. We are One. I AM forever in your heart and you in mine. This is the greatest lesson that I teach of all ~ to know that when you love Me, you love yourself. I knew this to be the Christ speaking again and remembered that I had asked Gretel to come and teach me. One of her greatest lessons had come when I had asked her to teach me, and so I had asked her to come again, as Teacher; *For I AM in you, and you in Me. Indivisible ~ We Are. The images of Gretel are as old photos with no life because the merge is complete. To say 'I am your Gretel' would be as empty words blowing in the wind. To say I AM, is all that can be said ~ and says it all.*

Thank you, Gretel. Thank you I AM, for all you taught me as Gretel. Tears welled behind my eyelids. I am ready for the next lesson.

And then, soon after this, suddenly, spontaneously, and all in the same instant, I experienced myself as a huge, vast, gigantic angelic being, and opposite me was another huge, vast, gigantic angelic being that I knew to be my Twin Angel, and down at our feet, delirious with joy and laughter was Gretel! Laughing and leaping and all but turning herself inside out with joy. *Oh, Gretel! You're not a dog at all are you?! You're an angel!* And I knew her as an emanation of my own Twin Angel come to bring me comfort and joy. And with eyes flashing, ears flapping and tail wagging every which way, Gretel redoubled her display of joy and delight that I had finally 'got it'.

~ ~ ~ ~ ~

The years went by, and of course I still thought about Gretel. And then one day, in my mind, I saw a Great Shaft of Light, reaching upward from the Earth to forever and beyond, it had no end that I could see, and I understood that Gretel was now a Wayshower to the stars for the animal kingdoms.

And then ~ seven years after Gretel's departure, friend Marilyn phoned in great excitement. Did I ever have a little dog called Gretel? Marilyn was a hypnotherapist, rapidly gaining tv and radio attention for her work with abductees. Marilyn dreamed she was on a ship, a star ship. She was standing beside a little being in a dome shaped room with a soft bluish white light, when she observed a small dog trotting by. This little dog had a mission, an assignment, she looked neither right nor left as she moved swiftly onward to her destination. "That looks like one of Sananjaleen's little dogs," said Marilyn in astonishment. She was familiar with Heidi and Tiggy and Loreli but she had not known Gretel.

"Yes," said the little being, who was about 4 ft tall, "That's Gretel. I'll show you where she works."

They followed Gretel down a long hallway, the walls appeared to be covered in hieroglyphs and lit by an intense blue light. Marilyn was still awed by the intensity of this little dog's purpose. Her coat shone (so shiny, so pretty), and she glowed with an etheric light. The little dog stopped in front of what appeared to be a door, waiting for it to open ~ and in she went. Marilyn and her escort stood in the doorway and viewed a room full of children. Sad and listless children, with sparse hair and pale skin. They sat around on floor and chair, with no apparent purpose. Gretel went straight to a particular child sitting on the floor. She licked its face, she climbed into its lap, she snuggled into its body, and she gave of her love ~ and the child began to perk and glow.

"She is teaching them about Love," said the little being. "She works at raising their vibrations and making them feel good. They need the love that she has to give them." A metallic suit covered his grayish skin. His eyes were big, black and round, his neck and arms long and thin. A belt buckle bore an insignia resembling the Star of David, with what seemed like a lightning bolt through the middle. Although his attitude was one of business and tour guide, Marilyn felt no fear or negative vibrations, she felt that he and his team cared about these hybrid children and wanted them to feel the love they were unable to extend themselves.

It wasn't hard to imagine the scene for Gretel had always loved everyone. Ever would she seek out, not the one who would give her the most love, but the one whom she could love the most. When she and Heidi visited the old people in nursing homes she shared her love equally amongst the patients, nurses, cleaning ladies, and administration staff, she opened their hearts and brightened their day with her love. Her ministry was recognized, and her presence requested at a time when animals were not freely accepted in such places.

Hybrid children. I was not comfortable with this expression. I didn't like the insinuation or the implication. In my own meditation I asked for clarification on this and was told they were 'children of the storm clouds'. I liked that better; it was more understandable. I could pretend these were Earth children who had been abused and mistreated, and now Gretel was loving them home, loving them free. And then, the following month, in the magazine *Connecting Link (issue #25)* I saw an article and picture of hybrid babies. That did it! I had to know what Gretel was doing! It was a long time since I had communicated with her, I simply no longer experienced her as a dog. Now it seemed that she had reactivated the Gretel-shell.

I have called for Gretel to come and explain more to me about who these hybrid children are, and her work with them. I see her in my mind's eye, my Gretel-dog, laughing and wagging her tail. It is a fine joke with her, playing this game, presenting herself to me as a dog again. She laughs! Her eyes shining, for she knows, and I know, that this is a game. She grows serious, her words flow telepathically through my mind;

But it is a necessary game. It is necessary because these children need help. They are the victims of war lords in that their right to freedom is curtailed, their choice diminished. Oh yes, at soul level there is agreement, but things may still get out of hand. Your planet is a planet of free choice, but these children are not on your planet. They are off planet. And different laws, different rules and regulations reign in different territories or dimensions. Children of the storm clouds, yes, for the storm rages around them. The rights and the wrongs, the do's and the do nots.

The freedom fighters would reclaim these children and set them free. In this case, releasing them from the form in which they are contained. And I ~ I AM there to help the children in whatever form they come. I nurture, I nourish that spark of love, that spark of light that is within them though they know it not. But they see the spark in Me. They see the love in MY eyes. They see the Light in MY Presence, and they respond. They respond because the Light is also within them. And in expressing, in acknowledging and claiming their right to feel do they grow. Do they grow out of the restrictions seemingly forced upon them. And the soul you see, knows the end result, but not necessarily every occurrence in between the agreement and the due date, the date due ~ because of variants and alternates and happenstance, and a multitude of ifs and whens.

Not every experience could be foreseen, and I ~ I AM here to help. To help the ones in childish form, to bring them comfort, to bring them remembrance, to bring a focus to their unlit minds. A purpose to their days of seeming lack of something worthwhile, of something to which they may respond, of something that would spark their intelligence, their knowingness, their inner guidance. For they sleep, these children, and it is Love that must awaken them, and this I came to do, and do.

And I will do this for all who call upon Me. For any who cannot sleep for lack of love, for any who cannot face the day because they feel redundant or unworthy, to them I come and bring My Love. And they may see Me how they wish. As an Angel I may enfold them in my wings, and as the dog you know, you knew ~ I would rest against their heart and have them hold me to their breast, and we would love each other. And their tears would water My joy, and My joy would grow because they cared for Me and held Me close. For in the giving would I receive, and in the giving would they know fulfillment.

Call to Me ~ call to Gretel the Angel dog, and she will come. And standing in the wings, excuse the pun, will be my Angel friends, and our Mother Mary ~ smiling, and holding this scene, this picture of compassion and treasured exchange within her Heart. Call upon me and I will come.

*For I AM here and I AM there. I AM everywhere present.
I AM an angel of the Lord Most High,
and as an angel ~ I can do anything,
from Gretel with Love.*

I already knew that Gretel was one of Mary's angels and was working with, for or through the Christ energy ~ or the Christ through her. How she does that is another matter altogether. And I wrote:

"I know without doubt, that Gretel is available to any who would call upon her in their hour of need, in our world or any other. I believe that she can be called upon to visit and share her love with any child, hybrid or human, to whom she is directed. The angel that Gretel truly is, works through the 'shell' or matrix of a long-haired dachshund, to express Divine Love in a manner unthreatening and acceptable to those whose inner lights are dimmed."

2023 ~ Thirty Years Later

On Easter Sunday, as I was doing my morning meditation
and declaring the portals of Sananda open, ready and available
to give and to receive the greatest Light possible,
I became aware of the entire Garden of Sananda,
the entire Sanctuary or Space of Love,
encompassed in a great blazing Golden Light
that I knew as *Gretel's Ascension Flame*.

The Ascension of Tiggy

March 1999

Smaller and younger than Heidi, Tiggy ran everywhere. She ran around the garden, she ran through rivers and up and down mountains. She ran in and out of bedrooms and up and down the corridors, around the table and under the chairs ~ all at top speed. It took her two years to learn how to stop. She usually came when called, but she didn't stop, she just kept on going! I used to call her *She Who Raced the Wind*.

Tiggy was seven years old when she joined Heidi and me, a week after Gretel died. Tiggy was a kennel dog, and never had a friend before. Heidi had never been alone. Gazing at Tiggy with loving adoration she said, *you're mine little Tiggy*, and Tiggy said, *I know big Heidi*, and they snuggled and cuddled and curled up together.

Having lived all her life with her mother, Heidi thought Tiggy was the most exciting thing she ever met. Tiggy taught her to hunt! Four hours at a time they sometimes went missing, but 'they', my inner guidance, would tell me when and where to expect the dogs back. 'They' even told me who would be in front, and by how many minutes. The accuracy was extraordinary and taught me to trust the inner guidance I was given with other information. I also learned to preface my questions to Spirit with 'as things are now', because sometimes Tiggy found another adventure between the time 'they' spotted her, and when she actually returned!

The two little dachshunds were inseparable, and as they nestled tightly together in their cuddler beds Tiggy remarked, *our hearts are beating as one. Heidi is teaching me to unite our breaths. I like it.* Heidi was teaching Tiggy to synchronize their frequencies, their heartbeats, to breathe as one so they could travel together in consciousness. Tiggy said that Heidi took her to *some very wondrous and amazing places*. One day after Heidi ascended, I asked Tiggy if she still visited these places. *Oh, no*, she said, seeming rather shocked, *Heidi told me never to go there without her. She said I might not be able to get back.*

In *The Lion People* by Murry Hope, there is indication that it is not safe to go travelling interdimensionally alone, without a guide. They speak of 'personal and God symbols' saying, "These are your safe conduct passes through uncharted time-zones, and without them you could encounter problems." The great Bulgarian spiritual Master Omraam Mikael Aïvanhov also warns of the dangers of interdimensional travel without appropriate awareness and spiritual understanding of what might be involved.

Meanwhile, Tiggy took advantage of Heidi's out-of-body training and started visiting people in their dream state! I asked her about this.

Heidi has taught me. Heidi doesn't visit people. Heidi soars out there. She joins Gretel, I know. Oh, I don't ask her what she does, but I know. She goes far. She will teach me. She's ready to help me do anything. But I like visiting people. And sometimes I visit these wild places where we go for walks. And I fly! I race over the stones and boulders. I tear across the land by moon light. Under the stars I run wild and free. And I am safe and happy and know I cannot get lost because my body waits for me, sleeping snug at home. It's exhilarating!

Who do you visit, Tiggy? Oh, I go see what Kate and Jane are doing (her two little dog friends). And Star (the neighbor's cat we sometimes pet sit). Star doesn't like it. He says it's very rude of me to come uninvited. But I go anyway. I curl up beside Mrs. Morf (Star's human) for a little bit. She's a nice lady. What was I doing with Christen? Christen had told me how Tiggy visited her in her dream state. I was practicing. I was thinking of all the nice people I know, and she was glad I came. I was very happy she was so pleased to see me. Mrs. Morf doesn't know I'm there. Sometimes I have to come back sooner than I want to, because my body wants to go outside. I love my body though it does cause me a bother when it itches so much.

What do you think, Tig? Are you ready to sleep now?

Not sleep, no. But I am ready to think my own thoughts, to myself. I love thinking in my little bed. I think about Heidi and how she loves me, and I think about that Gretel. I don't know what to make of her. I don't know what to make of Gretel either! Gretel and Tiggy never met in this lifetime.

One day a friend suggested that I ask Tiggy about her past. I knew that she had been leased out as a 'brood bitch', and that her breeder found her living in deplorable conditions, rescued her, nursed her back to health, and gave her to me.

> *There is no reason to remember.*
> *That was another's dream.*
> *My path has turned to Love,*
> *and I shall not stray.*

"Love keeps no record of wrongs." ~ Corinthians 13

"The things of the past shall not be remembered or come to mind. There shall instead be always rejoicing and happiness."
~ the Great Isaiah Scroll from the Dead Sea Scrolls discovered in 1947

I was sitting on the front steps, eyes closed in meditation. As she often did, Tiggy had wormed her way onto my lap and telepathically, like my own thinking, I heard;

This precious one represents Love made manifest in visible form. She represents the joy of action, love in action, delighting in all she encounters. Experiencing each new thing as it comes to her attention. Processing each new thought or feeling through her small being and letting it go, allowing it free passage through her own belief system. She recycles energies that may have become locked in their own patterns of belief or current existence ~ I am a bird, I am a mouse, I am a toad. She cuts them free! Free to live and build upon that they have known. Free to become one with the Light, the driving force that sparks them, that ignites them all ~ or free to enter a new experience, a new pattern of movement, a new rhythm of Light on the go. She keeps the love light burning strong. She keeps the God force active. God himself would become endangered were little ones like she to become stagnant and inactive.

Each living thing is a part of the whole, a cog in the universal wheel of life that rolls through time ~ that rolls beyond the timelessness of Truth as it unfurls, revealing ever new avenues of awareness, new dimensions of existence, new ages to explore and experiences to be. We bless this little one for she also serves the Light.

Tiggy had recently pounced upon and snuffed out the Light in a little mother mouse in the garage. The same with my very tame little white throated sparrow. And yet, I came to realize, there was only joy in her action, she was only sending fun and delight into the ethers. I was the only sad one! The other animals were accepting of entering into Tiggy's experiences. It was all the same to them, *hip, hop I'm a frog, skip, jump I'm a mouse, sort of thing.* I told myself that the small mother mouse had poured all her love and devotion and expectation into building her exquisitely perfect little nest, and that she might not have even liked her babies when they arrived!

And the little sparrow was so strange ~ running out of the bushes and over the grass for more bird seed whenever I left the house. Perhaps he was physically or mentally handicapped!

~ ~ ~ ~ ~

The garden itself continued to evolve. There is a labyrinth laid out on the grass in the vicinity of Heidi's Ascension Vortex. The area in the Pine trees beside it has become the Heidi Healing Center and brings peace, balance and harmony to all who enter. The dogs love to join me there. Tiggy likes to create a little nest for herself amongst the pine needles at the base of the tree nearest to Heidi's Ascension spot.

One summer's day as we sat there meditating together, my notes read: Miss Tiggy is 15 years old, and several months. Her eyes are not as clear as they once were, and her hearing has gone with the wind. She much enjoys coming here with me. Sometimes she curls up in the little nest she has made for herself in the pine needles and sleeps. Sometimes she just looks around ~ and around and around. All is well with her. She says;

As I mature, as you put it, and certain aspects of my functioning in this life withdraw, so do others come into focus and sharpen, to keep the balance. And where I once saw clearly with my bright and shining eyes, now I do see with my inner vision. And the pictures that I see are different than the ones I saw before. It is as though a curtain descends causing a refocusing of this vision, which allows for viewing of another dimension that is around. And these different dimensions express through frequencies, thus do they not interfere with each other. They exist within the one tone, but they express at a different vibration most finely tuned. And it does need practice. Much as those holographic images which are hidden within a picture, the focus must be exactly so to catch that inner world. And as the physical sight grows dim it allows for a concentration or awareness that other worlds are round about. It is the same with the hearing. I now hear different sounds than I did hear before.

I ask Tiggy if she will allow me to feel what she is feeling and seeing, and she says; *As you can see, I am busy. But if you wish you may share the experience.* I ask for assistance in expanding and developing my awareness of this. And just for a moment, a fleeting moment I do feel a great sense of being in the now. *That is all there is,* says Tiggy. *Just being here now.*

~ ~ ~ ~ ~

Suddenly ~ Tiggy was nearly 17 years old. She sleeps a lot and moves slowly. She loves her friends and visitors. She loves the fire and pottering around the garden on warm days. And the other dogs like to sleep with her, Loreli and Lorna and Candace. Whatever bed Tiggy chooses, the others pile in on top of her. She is their gateway to the stars, their pack leader, their treasured Elder. They seem to crave her presence, her energy. They have a need to be near her. The four little longhaired Dachshunds work as a team. Teachers and healers and active participants in all functions, workshops and playdays here at Sananda.

Her life seemed to ebb and flow. She had been sleeping most of the winter and seemed pretty much 'out of it'. Several people, myself included, figured she might be leaving pretty soon and we made funeral arrangements more than once! At that time, I had never heard of dementia, I just knew that Tiggy wasn't always enjoying her life. Sometimes the furniture blocked her walkabouts. Sometimes she could not find her way around a blank wall. And there were restless nights. And innumerable near-death experiences! *I'm going, going, going . . . OH! You just bought another roast chicken?! Well, I think I'll stay around a little bit longer!*

So I persisted with endless releasing ceremonies! For her and for me. I reminded her that Gretel had died peacefully in her sleep, why didn't she?! I just couldn't make that final decision to let her go, I had never done it before. Gretel and Heidi took care of their departure themselves. And I so wanted Tiggy to make it to her 18th birthday! I had arranged a party with a not-too-sweet carrot cake and all her presents would go to the local animal shelter. I was focusing on my wishes and wants rather than Tiggy's needs. So Tiggy took charge ~ and a week before her birthday she gave me two sleepless nights in a row! Zombie like, I called the veterinarian.

Eventually I understood that Tiggy was in a State of Grace and could have gone whenever she chose, but she wanted to give every last ounce of Service possible. She was my teacher. We had thought she might be leaving the previous summer. A group of friends had visited in the Springtime, and when someone invited Tiggy to sit in their lap, she wandered off to one of her little beds, rather shattering us all by announcing that the next time she climbed into someone's lap it would be to leave! So for the next few months, everyone was on tenterhooks whenever we gathered, watching to see whose lap Tiggy might choose! The same group returned mid-summer, and Tiggy told them that she was now rather sorry she had said that as she felt she couldn't sit in people's laps anymore! So we did a nice little releasing ceremony, just for Tiggy, absolving her from any vows, pledges or commitments she might have said or thought.

Meanwhile, I set an exercise during one of our Animal Communication Playdays asking Tiggy to give us her insights on growing old gracefully. She told Jan;

Leaving is sad but freeing, when you go you can really soar. There are certain qualities of spirit that never die but carry on. One of these is Breath. Not in the regular breathing sense, but in a fun breezy sort of way, I mean the Breath of Life. The sustaining life part, the thrill part, the soaking up kind of essence of heart. The thrill is the thing, that's what you take on and on into each new lifetime ~ Breath. Breathing it all in, taking it all in. Wishing it wasn't so that one thing had to end but realizing something new was going to begin ~ a new Breath! You just take an extra deep breath and when you let it out, there you are! On the other side.

" . . . a breath of love that takes you all the way to infinity". *~ Rumi*

"Breath is the bridge which connects life to consciousness, which unites your body to your thoughts." ~ *Thich Nhat Hanh*

And Drunvalo Melchizedek has described how, in a previous life, he and members of his Indian tribe left the planet consciously ~ *just by holding the breath.*

But before she started taking any extra deep breaths, I felt that Tiggy had something to tell *all* her friends. That she was preparing for transition and she had 'last words' for each. Not goodbyes, but words of wisdom and advice. Different for each. It was my job to alert these people, her friends.

Also, we hear much about a huge energy increase in consciousness this month, and I feel that Tiggy plans to ride this highly charged *Wave of Light Particles.* It is as if she has suddenly realized that although she enjoys being where she is, it is time to get on with things and start the next act. *Yes,* she says, *I'm packing my bags, before someone else has to do it for me.* She says this with some humor. And for a fleeting moment I wonder, is she catching the energy wave and riding high, or is she getting caught in the under tow? *Which do you think?* she snorts!

What is my role? What does Tiggy have to say to *me*? And she gives me a picture of both of us riding the crest of this immense wave. We are riding it together, braced to face what comes, crouched low to hold our positions ~ and then we are up, standing tall, riding the crest, and Tiggy moves swiftly onward and up, ahead of me, as a boat towing a water skier. She has great wings of Light, and says;

Once I was known as Race the Wind, now I am She Who Flies the Sky. I feel her as my mentor, someone for me to rely on, to give me strength and courage. She says; *Yes! I shall be your guide, and light your way as a beacon shining, bringing you home, bringing you to where I AM. And it is time for me to move. Enough is enough is enough, and I must make my move before it is made for me. My allotted time on Earth is drawing to a close, the curtain is already rising on my next act. These energies, these new Christed energies are the queue, you might say, for me to put my affairs in order. Affairs which include words of counsel and comfort to my friends and loved ones.*

Tiggy lived a long life and had a lot of friends! This assignment kept me busy all winter. Tiggy used the word friends, but I had the feeling she was being kind and polite, and that really, most of these friends were her pupils and chelas, following in her path. I started emailing all these friends of hers, saying; This afternoon Tiggy made me cry. She says, *I'm packing my bags*. And I told them what she had said and that she had a message, some 'last words' for each.

And she did indeed have very profound and meaningful messages for all. She came to them in dreams and meditations. One young lady, a well-known actress, credited Tiggy with 'saving her life' on account of symbolic guidance given in a dream. Another endearing young lady from England wrote two pages asking for Tiggy's 'last words' concerning her love life. Tiggy rather took the wind out of her sails by tersely replying, *marry him!* Tiggy took these things seriously, and after a few weeks, when this still hadn't happened, she told me to tell this young lady, *if you don't, somebody else will!*

Her friends called her the Wise One, the Wisdom Elder, and I asked that everyone send me a copy of the guidance received, so that I may make a compilation of Tiggy's Last Words!

~ ~ ~ ~ ~

And so, one bright and sunny spring morning, Tiggy ate today's *and* tomorrow's roast chicken for breakfast. She had a nice little sit in the garden, sniffing the breeze and watching the invisible kaleidoscope of colored lights and geometric patternings (the nature spirits and fairies), that mostly comprised the world in which she now lived.

A sweet and gentle veterinarian came at noon, and good friend, neighbor Neil came in the evening. We made a lovely nest of dried grass clippings and fresh rosemary, and laid the body, wrapped in a pretty cotton cloth, beneath the pine trees with a rose quartz heart resting on top. There is a statue of a silent master kneeling beside her, a large crystal cluster, a little tinkling fairy windchime, and an angel. It is a very nice place to sit, on all the soft sweet-smelling pine needles. And I did sit there the next day, with Loreli and Lorna and Candace ~ and it seemed just as though Tiggy was there with us. And I contemplated what she so often told me; *I am angel also. The fairy ones are Angelic too, forget not this.* I'm not sure when or why it started but I, and others, always called Tiggy our 'furry fairy'.

And then, a few weeks after her departure, I found some photos of Tiggy in the camera I forgot I had taken. Such joy! While waiting for the vet Tiggy was sitting outside in the sunshine. *So beautiful* she looked, her little gray face so peaceful, awaiting her appointment with Spirit in grace and patience. Serenity, Peace and Calmness in action. I called it Tiggy's Last Gift. And it did not dawn on me for many a month, that this scene, of Tiggy sitting outside beneath the big maple tree by the front door, with a small breeze blowing wisps of hair in her face, *was the exact same scene that friend Eva had seen in her meditations eighteen months earlier.*

Good friend Jamala wrote; "Tiggy came to me in my morning meditation, accompanied by Heidi. Such a feeling of joy and youthful exuberance. She is happy to be home and free, and sorry that she took so long to make up her mind!"

I sat beneath the pine trees and invoked the presence of precious Tiggy. I experienced faint impressions of her wiggling into my lap and kissing my face. She so loved our meditation times together, and it occurred to me to ask what she had felt during those last few minutes. What did you feel Tig? Can you share with me what you felt? Like Heidi did? Heidi had enabled me to experience the most incredible expansion in consciousness I ever knew. Words flowed through my mind;

It was a sudden quickening of my heart. The sudden realization of ~ this is it! It was very exciting for we did this together, her (Heidi) and me. It never occurred to me as a leaving or a goodbye, it was like the next step together, and Heidi was holding us both in her embrace, and that dear veterinarian felt it too ~ ask her. And then, for a while, it was like lying in the sun, on the beach. There is action, there is motion, as the waves come and go ~ but it was nothing to do with me. They did their thing, and I did mine, which was to bliss out, with Heidi around me ~ until I felt like doing something. And now I'm doing it. I'm helping Heidi full time. I don't know how she did it without me! What do you do Tig? Do you work with Gretel? *No. She's off on her own thing, not that we are separate or unaffiliated, but Gretel's spaceship is not my department.*

GRETEL HAS A SPACESHIP??!!! My mind ran wild with pictures of Gretel complete with goggles and scarf at the helm of a mother ship in deep space. Tiggy added kindly, *it's only a little one. A Gretel sized one.* Oh!

The young veterinarian had indeed been very moved, and remarked quietly how wonderful it was that we could do this for our animals, but not for our parents.

~ ~ ~ ~ ~

Tiggy seemed to be having a wildly joyful time in Spirit! She continued to take advantage of her training in entering people's dreams and went regularly to my Cherokee friend Spiritsong in her Tiggy-dog form, and in her waking state as a fairy, complete with tinkling fairy laughter riding on a physical dragonfly! She says she works with Loreli (who by this time had also returned to Spirit), and others. Working for the Earth, and all animals.

Spiritsong and I spent many happy hours on the telephone delighting in their playfulness and wisdom. I had never mentioned that Tiggy was our 'furry fairy', but she too was experiencing Tiggy in her fairy form! And without ever having seen them, she described the looks and mannerisms *exactly* of all the little dachshunds who often accompanied Tiggy in these dreams. Relating one dream she said;

"Tiggy came, and the beautiful dragonfly. Tiggy was in her Tiggy-dog form, bouncing and beautiful, shining and happy, very pleased with herself indeed. She mentioned again how busy they all were, and her promotion!" Spiritsong didn't know what she had been promoted to. I told her to go back to sleep and find out! She did! And Tiggy told her;

I'm in charge of all the dragonflies! She was thrilled. *Not Loreli! ME! I'm in charge of ALL the dragonflies! What are we doing? We're leading the birds to safety.*

In another dream, Spiritsong saw the beautiful dragonfly far out to sea over the ocean. Dragonflies don't belong in the ocean, she said, and in her dream, she heard the tinkling fairy laughter, a fairy giggle and a tiny voice say, *oh-oh!* And head quickly back to shore.

Yet again, Spiritsong phoned to say she had just seen a Monarch butterfly and heard the tinkling fairy giggle of our Tiggy. Shouldn't you be riding a dragonfly, she asked?

They're all busy, said Tiggy, *so I confiscated a butterfly!* Don't you mean, you 'commandeered' a butterfly, asked Spiritsong. *No,* said Tiggy, *I just took it!*

Contemplating all the joy and laughter Tiggy created for us, I tried to make reasonable sense of it all and heard;

The fairy isn't the whole of Tiggy, it's like her thought, her message. Her Love and Caring. She can do that because she is a central point for the fairies. A princess you called her, a furry fairy princess, but we see her as the eye of a vortex, an exquisite essence around which gathers the Beauty of Nature. In this case, Beauty depicted in the form of nature spirits or fairies.

And I 'knew' that the fairy flying around on the dragonfly that Spiritsong has recently seen physically, both times near her own little dog Georgette, was a sign to Georgette that her own departure time was very close, and I realized that Tiggy could send fairies flying around on dragonflies much as we would send a letter, a telegram ~ or text! Dragonflies have an agreement to act as 'horses' (or Ubers!) for fairies and take them wherever they need to go.

~ ~ ~ ~ ~

Still I questioned, what is Ascension? Can I say *The Ascension of Tiggy?* What exactly does 'Ascension' mean anyway? Clearly the answer came within my mind;

Indeed Tiggy ascended in spirit, in consciousness, back to the Eternal One. Very few of what you term companion animals do not ascend nowadays, for they are a High Order of Being that come to you in the first place. You, the 'chosen ones'. Chosen as you know, by yourselves, the chosen volunteers. And the definition of this Ascension is that they are drawn up, breathed back, rebirthed into the Truth of their Being, returning to Wholeness, to Oneness, to the Heart of God. Being once again who they truly are, with the ability to radiate throughout all levels and dimensions of consciousness, their love, their joy, their message of Hope. Going all the way, rather than just so far ~ the revolving doorway effect, which has been termed the wheel of karma.

Know that your Beloved Tiggy has ascended, and as with each that does, drawing others with her along the Golden Trail that shines in Glory like the Sun, with the ability now to do all things simultaneously and in full consciousness. A concept these Precious Ones in animal form would bring to your awareness, the awareness of those amongst whom they have lived and loved.

Tiggy taught the knowing of being responsible, of allowing life its Freedom. Tiggy could have gone any time she chose, but she chose to teach ~ through selfless Service and Love for you. She chose to empower you by the strength attained in making your own choice, your own decision. This strengthened her also. For it took much courage and strength to hold that Silver Cord, that River of Life connected. Your love helped and strengthened her of course when it grew frail and worn, it strengthened her determination to help you learn this lesson of detached Love, rather than clinging love.

Sitting beneath the pine trees, the thought has come to ask Tiggy if she has any more 'last words', and she says;

Teach people that animals have purpose too. As He who is the inspiration and Flame for us all once said, I too, must be about My Father's Business. And for those dear souls who baulk at a Father image, know that He spoke in the language of the day. And even if He did not, the translators, interpreters and teachers who followed surely did.

Today He might say something like ~ I must get on with my Soul's Mission. I must express the frequency that I AM. I must endeavor to stay in tune with Divine Intelligence, for I have come to embody and project the qualities of My Creator, the Father/Mother God ~ on Earth. Joyfully, in Grace and Gratitude. So Be It. And So It Is. Thus speak I, for all my companions who come in furry form ~ the one you knew as Tiggy, the Furry Fairy Princess.

Tiggy left us with many Eternal Truths,
insights and wisdom.
Where has Tiggy gone, where is she?
And I had the sense of unlimited vastness.
Spiritual limitlessness. *Tiggy is everywhere present.*
No longer She Who Raced the Wind but ~ She Who Flies the Sky.

The Ascension of Loreli

September 1999

Exquisite and petite, I likened her to fine bone china, porcelain perfection. Loreli joined Heidi and Tiggy and me when she was seven years old, a Champion of Champions in the Show Ring. Loreli thrived on secrets and excitement and would undoubtedly prefer an entire book to herself, but I will limit this segment to the activities surrounding her transition and comments on Ascension. Visitors were acknowledged by Loreli racing through the house shouting, *the aliens are coming, the aliens are coming!* Eventually it dawned on me that *she* was the alien. She was our little ET, our space gnome, a Sun of the Sun, a Cosmic Dolphin, and The Wave. 'An extra-terrestrial master of energy control', as one friend described her. She supervised our Animal Communication Playdays, she kept us on track, and for years we all quoted 'what Loreli said'!

Every year I plant little seedlings, small plants, in the veggie garden. Tomatoes, zucchini, eggplants, peppers ~ I could never understand why they all died and/or disappeared. I assumed it was the birds, nipping them off at ground level. This went on for a long time, until one day, as I returned with the watering can to sprinkle four little freshly planted baby peppers ~ only one was still standing. The other three lay neatly nipped and sadly dead on their sides *and Loreli was walking away from the fourth*, trying not to hurry, trying not to look guilty, but knowing full well she had been caught in the act! Not a word was said, but it never happened again. Once her secrets were discovered Loreli moved on to new ones.

Eventually I had the veggie garden fenced in, just a low wooden trellis to keep the little dachshunds from helping themselves and that I could easily step over. They watched in silence, radiating disapproval and condemnation. Job complete, Loreli wasted no time in poking her head through the lattice work and rolling her eyes at me with an expression that said, *Look! Look what you've done to me! I can't move! I'm stuck!* I phoned good friend and neighbor Neil to come with his box of tools and cut her free.

Come fall, I planted bulbs, daffodils and tulips. The very first time I did this, I discovered that Heidi was following along behind me digging them all up! Knowing that Loreli would probably do the same I planned to shut her in the house, but she was stretched out asleep on the deck and I was headed down to the other end of the garden, so I left her in peace. I had already shut Lorna and Candace in the house so they wouldn't see what I was doing and at seventeen years old, Tiggy was no longer a threat. The ground was brick hard and it took me an hour or so. I headed back to the house and saw that Loreli was still stretched out fast asleep on the deck. HA!

I just happened to glance back through the window at the very moment she was hurrying down the porch steps and speedily heading towards the newly planted bulbs! She had watched my every move and made her own plans from between the deck railings. LORELI! I roared, *come here!* And with exquisite nonchalance, she made a sweeping half circle and trotted back to the house, casually tossing her head and glancing at me through half closed *'I wasn't doing anything'* type eyes. She does so hate to have her secrets found out.

And then one day as I sat for my morning meditation beneath the pine trees, Loreli joined me and very gently, so very gently, touched my arm with her little paw and gazed hesitantly into my eyes. Would she speak? Tightly I held her; *I merge with this one in my arms, I merge and unite with her at heart level.* I see her bright and shining eyes peering out of her little pointed face. It is Loreli's face and yet ~ it is merged with the picture of an alien, a Pleiadian, on the front cover of Sedona Journal of Emergence (Vol 2 No 12). Loreli's bright black eyes merge into the great blue ones in the painting ~ and I call forth the Holy Christ Self of Loreli, if there is such a thing. My spine tingles and words come;

In this case there is, and this one comes to you in gentleness, and this one comes to you in love. And this one comes in trust that it would be taken care of and protected, and given a base from which to operate, to perform its task in canine form. No dog is this one, from the far, far distant star systems she comes. Through the Pleiades yes, but not from.

Her race is a race of very gentle beings who are not familiar with the physical form, being contained within the canine form, and thus it is she appears wild and overly jubilant at times. It is hard for her to adjust, to contain her energies in such a very small and compact frame. No great frame has she herself in her own domain, but she and her kind have the capabilities of expanding it, expanding their sensations so that they feel they are vast beings, as indeed they are.

They expand themselves, and merge with one another in their expanded state and operate as one, retracting to their individual form, their individual selves to go about their daily business, their daily lives. And this expanded form, this merged essence might be described as community living. And so it is hard for her to remain continually in the contracted form without the release of the expansion, the merged essence. In her dream state of course she is free, otherwise it would be impossible for her to hold to this pattern without shattering.

Her job? To assist, as all have come, to assist. She was the one who volunteered and was chosen to be an extension of this system. What is her focus? What did she come to do? To be here. To be here. 'We want to help too' was their heart's desire, 'we want to help too'. And so we sent our finest and our best and purest of heart to dwell amongst you and raise your consciousness by our presence. To raise your vibrations through feeling our love.

And so great was the Love I felt that emotional tears of overwhelm flowed copiously down my cheeks.

We have no gallant battle to play, to fight, for we see your fights as play, destructive play, and we hoped that by living amongst you we could awaken the joy of living in you, teach you to express the gaiety and freedom that is the inherent right of each by watching our gaiety and joyfulness, our freedom of expression, our dance through life. We thought perhaps you might take note and join us, and share with us our enthusiasm, our appreciation, and our love for the life our Creator has given to us, to you, to all who are in form. To all who have consciousness. This one has spoken.

She has the support of her own kind, beamed to her you might say. This is the only way we can present a picture to you of how she receives the support of her own kind. No, they have not incarnated upon your Earth before, and never, or if so, very rarely as an experiment, in human form. It would be too hard for them. It would be too hard. They can only come in a loving form that must also receive constant love in order for it to exist. Without this love, this replenishment, they would simply fade away and not be.

Her team, the support team with which she is in contact in her sleep, is stationed upon the Pleaides, and send blessings to you and give thanks that you care for one of us in such a loving manner. Allow her to express this love, our love, her freedom, our freedom, to choose with whom and where we may exchange our joy in as many ways as possible, and she shall fulfill our hopes. The hopes of her community, her homeland, her own land.

I asked that when her time came to leave this planet, that it would be in gentleness and love.

Be assured that when the time comes we shall withdraw her essence with great gentleness. We shall help her slip out of her form as she sleeps, in great peace and joy at our reunion, at her welcome home. She shall be given such a mighty (floods again), *welcome when she returns to her homeland. And Loreli, her name, expresses the quality of her essence so well. We thank you and offer you the blessings of her people ~ and we withdraw our energies.*

A German interpretation of Loreli's name is 'alluring enchantress'!

~ ~ ~ ~ ~

One day a friend visited who became very flustered and upset by the four little dachshunds and their enthusiastic welcome, saying she was allergic to them. After she left, I asked the dogs to form a group energy, a synergy and speak as one. I asked for their commentary on why she had seemed so unreasonably affected by them. Loreli stepped forward immediately (symbolically, in my mind), and said, *she was not allergic to us, she was allergic to what she thinks we represent.* And I was given a picture of wolves. A beautiful scenario as from a scenic postcard, but these wolves were alive and moving. Loreli continued:

She thinks we represent the canines. The canine family. The wild ones of the woods she feared so much. And yet we came to sing to her, to bring her companionship. But she could not hear our song. She allowed the fear that was in her heart to take over. Fear for herself, her safety dominated her thoughts and actions. And we would sing to her more loudly that she may hear the message we would give. But it could not be and so we went our way and left her. And loneliness engulfed, and she did miss this nightly chorus that she had come to be in expectation of. And now she was torn between loneliness and fear.

And the little ones did bring her great comfort (the small woodland animals), and in the daytime, she could pretend they were all she needed. But in the nighttime, she was sore afraid, and these fears built into a cloak that surrounded her and penetrated within each cell, and this remembrance was brought to the surface, for our presence reminded these cells of group energy. Group energy that sang to her, and in their feeling tones we sang to her once more and they knew not how to accommodate our song. And they released their passionate emotions, so long held in storage.

And if you would give her words from us that would assist, then we would say to her to understand it was a release. And she need no longer fear adverse reactions from the canine form, for these memories are gone. Swept by the wind and rain into the ethers where they may be recycled to a higher purpose, and a freedom they have not known for quite some time.

And we would bless her, this one, for allowing herself to come and be cleansed of their infringement upon her person and her way of life. And we would say, we would suggest that she do some ceremonial follow up to this release. Flower essences we would say, would be the most appropriate way of cleansing the vibratory patternings that have been opened now, and might be in need of purification and statement of intent filled with purity and love.

And who are we who speak? We are the spirit of those who sang to her one time so very long ago when she was lonely and afraid.

I gave thanks and asked what connection Loreli had with those who have spoken, and I was told, *ask not the secret of the singing stars, ask not of worlds not your concern.*

~ ~ ~ ~ ~

Less than six months after Tiggy's transition, Loreli developed a very fast-growing abdominal tumor. She gave me two days to fulfill her last wishes. Ever the teacher, she wanted 'her group' united, she wanted to demonstrate the Power of Prayer, to show them what they can do when they work together. She wanted me to alert all her friends, nationwide, to light a candle and meditate at 9 pm on Friday night, holding the vision of Loreli *'Dancing in the Light'*.

The other dogs did not appear concerned. This was Loreli's thing, and I was accustomed to obeying her commands! So many times had she come to me during the animal communication playdays, dancing in front of me, to and fro, back and forth ~ placing her tiny paw upon my knee, gazing intently into my eyes until I *'got it'*. Until I listened to her and heard what she had to say, what she wanted me to tell the others.

Loreli had lots of friends, so I was busy on the phone and with emails. All her friends, coast to coast, honored her request and held the vigil to see Loreli *Dancing in the Light.* Some cancelled previous engagements, dinner dates even. Everyone had beautiful stories to tell and did indeed see her dancing in the light, amid pink and golden swirls and spirals of radiant energy. Friend Amy was having dinner with the veterinarian who read the laboratory tests and had never meditated before, they both saw Loreli immersed in a pink flame, laughing with the butterflies!

Meanwhile, during her afternoon meditation, Marilyn, who had been staying with the little dachshunds while I was away, experienced a beautiful pink vortex of Divine Love being generated from Loreli's Heart. "She prepares it now for all who will be joining us tonight as the energy of compassion and unconditional love is poured forth from all directions. Loreli has orchestrated this, not just for herself, for she has not yet made a decision whether she will dance into the Light and make her transition or use this embrace of Love to receive miraculous healing. She has created this Vortex of Love to also affect all who are giving to her in this Service of Light. I feel the vortex like a funnel streaming upward from her heart. It is tilted, and I suggest righting it so that it is over her, and she says; *no, it is not time, that will happen tonight when all are with me. Then it will expand and touch all the hearts of those who come in Love to be with me. Then I will be at the base or center of this vortex.*

It wasn't until later that evening, during the *Dance of Light* meditation, that we understood how much more this was all about, that Loreli was creating or opening a portal to take many, many animals with her into the Light."

Marilyn and I dressed in white and filled the room with candles and crystals and watched as Loreli, seemingly rather restless, moved from one little bed to another before she settled on her favorite beanie bag. Each time she changed position, Lorna and Candace moved with her. Marilyn continued:

"The Pink Vortex is indeed upright now, rather like a spiral with Loreli at its base. The original circle of 13 (Loreli's local 'group') are enveloped in it, and as they simultaneously give and receive the vortex expands greatly. Then come the Rays of Light from those out of state and coast to coast, forming the next ring of Loving Light. Sananjaleen has invited all animals who wish to come through this Vortex of Love and make their own transition-ascension. Oh, so many, many come, injured, frightened, lost, all gratefully moving through this awesome portal of Love. Quan Yin's exquisite energy of compassion is overlighting all of this.

And I remember the beautiful portal of transition that is being held open here at Sananda by Mother Mary, Quan Yin, and the Angels of Transmutation and Transition. It formed two days ago for those of East Timor (an earlier meditation we held for the multitude of animals, elementals and humans affected by the widespread violence in that country). There are two vortices, Loreli's nested inside the other, a central vortex of pink, surrounded by a golden white glow, seemingly opening to different dimensions, and yet both serving the gift of a peaceful shift of frequencies into the Light. I am so blessed to be a part of this. Loreli tells me;

If I choose to go and don't take my body with me, that doesn't mean I didn't ascend. Some ascend and don't take their bodies. Either because they did that before, or don't need them ~ it is a personal thing.

Just before closure we asked that this Vortex be sustained in Spirit as long as needed, and I saw Loreli joyfully ascending into the exquisite Pink Light ~ *and she didn't dance alone!* What a beautiful orchestration of Service and Love by this precious being called Loreli, who was now resting very peacefully in her little bed."

Loreli stayed with us through the weekend, and on Monday morning the same sweet young veterinarian who had assisted Tiggy, came to help her release from the physical body. Marilyn held Lorna, special friend Sharon came to hold Candace, and I held Loreli. We sat in a circle on the sunlit floor with a gentle breeze blowing through the open windows, activating the windchimes and sending dancing rainbows darting through the crystals and flickering all around. And just as her Team had promised, *Loreli slipped from her sleeping form in gentleness, peace, and love.*

~ ~ ~ ~ ~

There is an area in the garden I call the Gnome Sanctuary, and while meditating there the day before Loreli departed, the gnomes had informed me; *We want Loreli!* Normally, I would have placed her body in another area, with Tiggy. But we honored their request. Neil was away, so Marilyn and Sharon created a space big enough for an Irish Wolfhound, or so it looked to me! They looked surprised when I suggested enough already! Standing up to admire their work they felt it was just the right size ~ so we all knew Loreli was still in charge!

I felt that somehow, Loreli embodied the Wisdom of the Buddha, that it was lodged in her bones, and that the gnomes could now access this knowledge, and radiate this frequency far and wide. When meditating here the next day, the gnomes gave me images of themselves busy with their little wheelbarrows ~ coming and going with great reverence and joy, taking something, an essence, from Loreli's body which was buried in their domain. It seemed like a long awaited and eagerly anticipated event. It reminded me of the importance that some place on the relics, the bones of saints.

~ ~ ~ ~ ~

Such a beautiful day. I sat beneath the Pines in Heidi's Ascension spot, and asked Loreli if she had anything to say; *I AM everywhere present!* Oh! Well! Is there a name for this everywhere? *Heaven!* Oh! And I thought rather vaguely of a huge expanse of golden vastness. How could someone visualize where their animal might be? And I was given the idea that one only has to hold the thought of whatever it is one wants for the animal ~ to do, or be, or go, and it would be so. Many people 'see' images of their animal, passing over a rainbow bridge or happily well and youthful again. Loreli continued:

We give you these images or impressions for your own understanding, peace of mind and delight, that you may question and learn more. They are to show that we are in a state of peace ourselves. In appropriate surroundings for our comfort and joy. That we are well and happy and learning more, not just blissing out in a state of grace. We love you so much and we want you to understand that we are so much more than we appear to be when we come into your lives as dogs or cats or coyotes. Each incident and interaction of our lives with yours has meaning. Has intent. Has a reason and purpose, as do we ~ your beloved companions. Not always quite so beloved it would appear to some, but none the less, we would not be in your lives were it not that your soul has called us forth. I speak for all. I speak to all. I am Loreli ~ Master Teacher in Love and Joy.

She certainly was speaking in a very different tone than the 'old' Loreli. Lorna came to sit in my lap, grieving for her beloved little companion. Gazing sorrowfully into my eyes she said, *remember the living. It can be very hard for those of us who remember* (what Heaven is like).

That evening, I sat to meditate upon Loreli. I could visualize her so clearly, dancing around being busy, busy, busy, with her special 'I've-got-a-secret' look. But I must think of her as she is now, not conjure up scenes from the past. Words come;

I too have cleared. I am activating people. They all need activating! I work with them in their dream state. There are only a few who can work with me consciously. I work with all who have ever heard my name or seen my face ~ that gives me entrance to their energy field. And their energy fields to me are like gardens. And some have flowers that need water and encouragement. And others have seeds they have forgotten or don't know how to plant. I help them. I have kept my body. I love my little body! It's a very handy size. It doesn't scare anyone.

Do you work with Tiggy and Heidi?

Heidi overlights us. We work within her Radiance. Tiggy works with people too, but she is more of a stabilizer, holding the balance and focus. She goes only when she is needed. I go whether the people know they need me or not! Jamala, he needs us. Tiggy is working with him. I just go along for the ride, it's an opportunity for us to be together.

On another occasion, Loreli repeated that she works with anybody who has ever seen her face or heard her name, adding, *Tiggy only works with those who ask!*

During the next six months or so, I received a series of telephone calls from people telling me about a little dachshund who came into their dreams, or they walked into a bookstore and a book fell open at page 122, displaying a photo of Loreli and Tiggy (*Communicating with Animals* by Arthur Myers). Each was seeking help regarding their own little dog who had made or was about to make its transition. Gently I would interrupt their ramblings to ask if this little dog was a dachshund and if it had a tumor. Yes, and yes! They all thought I was an amazing psychic and/or medical intuitive. Alas no, I just knew Loreli very well!

Linda Rose reported that as she was asking her angels for guidance she heard; *There are many of us here with you, my name is Loreli. Recently I was embodied as a dog who lived with Sananjaleen, she is very dear to me and I am glad you will be taking care of Candace and Lorna.*

Linda had a very old car and was asking for guidance as to whether she should travel from Florida to Virginia to do this while I was away. She had not heard Loreli's name before.

Attie in Aruba wrote; "Yesterday in my meditation I saw a lovely little dachshund head with the most beautiful eyes that asked me what's my problem. I told her, addressing her as Loreli and later said, sorry was that Heidi? But whoever it was said not to worry." Attie also had never met any of the little dachshunds, she had only heard about them via email.

Like Tiggy, Loreli was very active in the dreams of my Cherokee friend Spiritsong who kept connecting with people who mentioned a little dachshund. She thinks Loreli is energizing them with her spirit spark. Loreli takes Spiritsong herself through 'doorways' or portals in her dreams and meditations. Often they emerge into a glorious forest or golden meadow and meet with various Ascended Masters. At other times Spiritsong is shown gatherings of animals receiving instructions for helping the Earth in her Ascension process ~ frequently with Loreli as the 'Commander-in-Chief'! And although Spiritsong never saw her physically, she describes Loreli's character, her actions, her looks, her ways, her petiteness, and the little toss of her head and 'squinty eye' look *exactly*.

Such a glorious, glorious morning. I am sitting beneath the Pines, thinking of Loreli and her work in Spirit. She and Georgette (one of Spiritsong's little dogs) have been 'on assignment' and Spiritsong was shown them in a dream, lying stretched out on the grass, resting in Golden Light. Who is Loreli really? I wondered. And what is she to me exactly? And I see her within my heart, sitting in the deepest chambers of my heart, much like a tiny bronze Buddha I have that sits within an amethyst geode, as if in a temple cave.

Loreli is the Buddhic Essence within your life. She lives within your heart. Your Heart activates her. If your heart closed to her ~ she would not exist. Her Essence is forever, but her playfulness as Loreli is kept alive by you. Her work in the outer realms would continue, but as formless emanations. What would happen to the Garden and the Spiritsong dreams and visions? If your heart closed, your world would close and all within it would disperse, evaporate, and folding in upon itself like a set of dominos, this world would end. Thus may you know, every thought and action that you have affects the entire Universe. One world the less, may not affect the Universe so adversely, you might think. But has it not been said, that every sparrow is counted in the Heart of its Creator?

Thus is it so for each, and every world is known and loved and needed for the completion of Existence, that Existence may complete itself and be reborn, in ever higher and finer frequencies. Ascension, you term it. Ascension in a very basic form compared to what we speak. Child's play dear one, in view of that to come! And so, keep your heart open that your world may blossom and bloom to maximum potential, and when all worlds are in full bloom shall the Creator gather these glorious colors, and sort them into radiant bouquets, Gifting Himself-Herself for His-Her own Creative Play.

And then Loreli went to my friend Ingrid and revealed that her name was now 'Loreli-Li'. Neither of us had any idea what this meant. Later I 'heard'; *Loreli is a multi-dimensional Being with full consciousness of this. Her new title or name, Loreli-Li, denotes awareness or recognition of her Service as she expands into other realms, other universes. Your Loreli is of the purest Light.*

Regarding the comment that she loved her little body, Loreli said that she had remodeled and updated it so that she could swim underwater with the dolphins! And gave me an image of the ocean, and far out to sea in the middle of nowhere was a high diving board with Loreli standing on top! And in she dove. Tail and ears streaming back in the wind, eyes tight shut, little nose resting on outstretched paws. Totally free. Unrestricted in thought or deed. *That's what Ascension is!* she says and reminded us again ~ *one can also Ascend after leaving the body.* And I had the thought that Loreli had probably already mastered the Ascension process on her own planet. She can take any form she wants, but she loves her little Loreli body! Rather like a favorite car in the garage.

Also, there is a very powerful photograph, a commanding pose Loreli herself created as she sat upright just behind one of the Buddha statues in the garden and gave me the impulse to turn around and click the camera. This picture had such impact on those who saw it that I printed a hundred postcards, and Loreli adorns refrigerators and office desks worldwide! And still, twenty-five years later, people ask for poster size prints!

A friend showed this photo to one who works with Saint Germain. "Yes," he said, "people think they are dogs, but they are highly, highly evolved benevolent beings. Many of them come from Sirius." Of Heidi he said, "Exactly, they can leave however and whenever they want." And my Chinese acupuncturist, on viewing the photo of Loreli and Buddha murmured, "Buddha's last incarnation perhaps?!" This image of herself on display makes it easier for Loreli to continue her work in this dimension, with a specific person or people, or particular place.

And then one day as I stood absentmindedly in front of this photo, I had an overwhelming flash of Cosmic Understanding. Suddenly, all in the same instance, I experienced Loreli, my precious little miniature longhaired dachshund, existing simultaneously on all levels and dimensions at once, expressing in each at the same time. Somehow, she was an energy of great importance, a force of empowerment to the gnomes in the garden, who had asked for her body to be placed in their sanctuary, that her crystallized emanations may bless and work with them and the land. She was my precious little dog; a Being from her far-off planet; an extraterrestrial Master of Energy Control ~ a Star Commander?! An angel? But I received no impressions of angels. I saw only a vast and dazzling, brilliant sphere of fiery golden Light ~ with a small and brilliant fiery Sun zipping in and out of it. Loreli is a Sun of the Sun! And I understood that I too exist simultaneously on all these levels, a Sun of the Sun that can come and go as, when and where needed.

> *Even if you were to know yourself*
> *as the most evolved chakras or advanced Light Vehicles,*
> *you would be limiting yourself*
> *if you did not fully know yourself first*
> *as a formless Sun of expanding Cosmic Consciousness.*
> *All around you, great Cosmic Beings*
> *traveling at the speed of Light*
> *traverse this matrix,*
> *emerging in and out of these Suns.*
> *~ Group Avatar*

> *Truly the Mighty I AM Presence is a Sun of the Sun,*
> *but we are equally an extension of this truth,*
> *an embodied Sun of the Sun when immersed*
> *in our Eternal Flame and its Infinite Radiant Light.*
> *~ Ascended and Free*

> *Representing every embodied soul is a Sun of the Sun.*
> *The Mighty I AM Presence projecting its Divine Presence*
> *into the physical, etheric, mental and emotional realms*
> *of daily life ~ as the Solar Christ Self.*
> *~ Ascended and Free*

And an image of a poster I once had came to mind, of the Earth as seen from space, encircled by two great dolphins. And I was given to understand that Loreli was also a Cosmic Dolphin. At this point I needed time out! I phoned Spiritsong and told her that I had seen Loreli as a huge dolphin, a Cosmic Dolphin, one of several holding the Earth in their embrace, had I got that right? Next morning she phoned to say; "After we talked, I got so sleepy, my eyes closed, and I fell sound asleep. The following message came through from Loreli with Georgette at her side:

I am indeed the Dolphin, but I am also the Wave. I am the sunlight and the moonlight. I am multidimensional, serving on many levels, always where there is a need. Look to the Flame and its layers of color and brightness, surrounding the core or heart. That is Me. We are of this world, but not of this world. We are the pure energy of Love that lights the Way. Keepers of the Flame. Question less and believe more. You honor us with your love. There are many changes to happen, and soon. Energy is shifting as I speak. Don't be afraid. Speak our names and we will be there.

According to quantum physics 'wave function' means the state of all possibilities, the act of human observation collapses or 'freezes' that part observed into particle form. Loreli loved being observed, acknowledged and 'recognized'! She was a fine example of the following;

*Elemental Life fulfilling their Divine Potential
of expressing 'wave function' Perfection Patterns
in 'particle function' form!* ~ Ascended and Free

Here in part, is the response of U.S. Naval Commander William S. Buehler after I related to him that Loreli said she was not only the Cosmic Dolphin, but also The Wave.

"The Cetacean is the 13th sign in our Universe's zodiac, it rides the Wave of Love. The Cetacean will be replaced by the Unicorn in the Metatronic zodiacal upgrade as the Christos in Nature. The dog relates to Sirius in the triunity of Sirius, Orion, and the Pleiades (including Alcyon, Central Sun), also to the 'Shepherds' or Solarians, and Thoth as the Anubis. It seems to me that the dog, Sananjaleen's little Loreli that correlates with / as the Cosmic Dolphin is a combined dynamic for the Solarian working in the 13th Sign.

'Loreli' sits on a large Stone in the Rhine, singing to sailors, a Siren. She would represent the ability to replace destructive codes (in vocal sound) to Metatronic Harp music where the human is the range of strings responding to Spirit/Grace. The River is Time, or the Mighty Wave, or the Metatronic Ranna Wave relating to Unity Consciousness."

~ ~ ~ ~ ~

Six years later, I was still telling Heidi, Tiggy, and Loreli stories, and the thought came that she (Loreli), was a Keeper of the Stargate;

In the fullness of her Essence she is vaster than that with which you have as yet connected or even imagined could be. Another dimension altogether. And in her vastness, Loreli is actually Guardian of the Portal or complex of Star Systems which only now open into or are brought to your awareness. Loreli is the feminine energy personified in one you recognized as 'exquisite as fine china', a porcelain Madonna in canine form! Energies associated with the Magdalene. Multi diversified and complex in the extreme (smile) are the qualities behind the purpose of your 'pet dogs' love and meaning in your life. Do all dogs have such agendas? All dogs do not carry such agendas or resonate with such Beings or Qualities, but the dog nature allows embodiment of these Masters and/or Qualities as and when required.

And I recalled a meditation in which I had been given the understanding that Loreli was also a Wormhole! Google implies that Wormholes are just theoretical, no one has ever actually seen one, they are just mystical hypothetical musings. Sounds like just the sort of thing Loreli would like to be, to me!

Oh Loreli! How I love you!

The Ascension of Lorna and Lilly

October 2004

Lorna joined us at seven years old. From the moment she arrived, Lorna programmed me with her beautiful laughing eyes to believe that she was nothing but pure love and sweetness, a little dog who could and would do nothing 'wrong'. She made me believe that she was almost boring she was so 'good'! She gave this impression to others too, "Lorna is always such a well-mannered and proper lady", they said. What a bunch of baloney!

She was pure Love alright. She was also a fun-loving con artist, subtly outrageous in her deeds. We had a lot of potlucks, playdays and presentations in those days and the little dachshunds loved them all. Lorna had taught herself the most endearing Sit-up! With no warning or apparent reason, she would suddenly do one of her Sit-ups! Perfectly balanced on her rear end, she would sit bolt upright and gaze lovingly at her 'victim'. It was always a major conversation stopper. She specialized in doing it in front of a small, seated group, each with something delicious on their plate. Once she relaxed from her sit-up people went back to chatting, and with lightning speed and precision, Lorna would grab the last bite off her selected plate! The unfortunate target never knew what happened. Staring at their empty plate in bewilderment, no one ever thought to suspect Lorna, who by this time was doing another Sit-up in front of her next victim. She also specialized in opening things ~ like garbage and grocery bags. She also led the pack in ripping open a 40lb bag of birdseed in the back of the car. The only thing she couldn't open was a watermelon.

She conned a professional animal communicator into thinking she was a cat and the poor woman made ridiculous suggestions regarding changing her kitty litter and other cat related recommendations (this via a remote consultation). And to a dear friend who stayed with the pack when I was away, Lorna had her believe that she had been rescued from a circus. Although perhaps her depiction of a dog show could be interpreted as such, for Lorna had been a Champion of Champions in the Show Ring.

As far as I was concerned, Lorna taught in silence. For the next nine years, try as I might, I could seldom 'hear' what she might have to say. To my persistent, 'why won't she speak to me, why can't I hear her' demands, I always received the thought, *consider that Lorna holds her silence.* Lorna was teaching me to 'go direct' to my own inner knowing, without seeking information, approval or *fun* from others. I was a stubborn, resistant and reluctant pupil. Lorna was equally stubborn and relentless ~ and held her silence.

But during our Animal Communication Playdays she was a gentle and loving teacher in helping her 'class' practice their inter-species communication skills. To someone who asked what some of her favorite things were, she replied, *springtime and babies! I saw one the other day, it came out of a box on wheels, but it was a baby alright. A human baby!* This person had no way of knowing that the previous week a young mother had brought her baby into the garden, and lifted him out of the stroller to smell the flowers. Another participant who asked her about her past, said, *Lorna keeps showing me a picture of herself standing on a little table, and I don't know what it means.* This person didn't know that Lorna was a Show Dog, and because dachshunds are so little, they get photographed with all their trophies standing on a table! Someone else was having a difficult time as her last child was leaving for college. Lorna responded to her plea for help with the poignant words, *you have to let them go. Even though I know I will never see my puppies again, I will love them forever and always.*

~ ~ ~ ~ ~

Seven years later, Lorna's daughter Lilly joined us. She was supposed to have joined us in the spring, but transportation problems involved much shuttling around in crates, hours on the road and the last five weeks in a Beagle kennel. Lilly arrived starved for love, joy and exercise. She wasted no time in giving and receiving all three! She was joy in action, and something as simple as tying my shoelaces became a major accomplishment as Lilly came racing over to lick my face. I took to resting my foot on the table, but Lilly would leap into the armchair, jump onto the table, race through the plants and smother my face in happy kisses! Casing the food pantry was a favorite sport of Lorna's, but Lilly could actually jump up on the first shelf and create even bigger and better disasters. And she was *so* ecstatically happy to be re-united with her mother, she didn't want to let Lorna out of her sight.

> "Entreat me not to leave thee,
> or to turn from following after thee,
> for whither thou goest, I will go;
> and where thou lodgest, I will lodge."
> ~ *Ruth verse 16*

Lorna would curl up in the smallest bed available, hoping there was no room for another dog, but Lilly would simply climb in on top of her, sometimes balanced against the couch behind them. It wasn't hard to imagine Lorna saying, *daughter, I'm meditating*, and Lilly responding, *mummy, mummy, I'll meditate with you!* Or, *daughter, I'm trying to sleep*, and Lilly responding, *mummy, mummy, I'll sleep with you!* Rather unkindly, I reminded Lorna of her remark about loving her puppies forever and always, she broke her silence long enough to retort, *that was then! This is now!*

Lilly specialized in Bag Investigations. She was declared of Olympic Standard. No sooner did anyone enter the house and deposit their bag, whatever sort of bag it was, than Lilly was in it. Candace and Lorna sat beside her knowing she would retrieve anything of interest, and Lorna was once heard to murmur that her manners must have come from the father's side, *I had nothing but perfectly behaved children*.

Soon after her arrival Spiritsong, my Cherokee friend, phoned to say, "Lilly came to me in a dream last night, she was surrounded by white Light and said, *I'm all brand new!* I asked her, what does that mean? She said, *I'm brand new means I'm brand new!* When asked anything else (in the dream), or regarding her purpose in coming, she simply repeated, *I don't know! I don't know yet because I'm brand new! Loreli would know!* And then, after a while she volunteered, *the Lightworkers created me. They just made me!*"

> Looking into Lilly's eyes I know;
> *She comes from the future.*
> *From the limitless void of unknown choice,*
> *the ocean of glory unformed,*
> *the treasure that waits our discovery.*
> *Lilly comes as dawn heralds the day,*
> *as gentle waves break lightly on the sand,*
> *before the tide has turned.*
> *She comes as an angel of hope and encouragement.*

Perhaps when Lilly spent time in 'hospital' being spayed before she came to us, she was cleansed of her past, purified, and when she awoke, she felt as though she was born again ~ *all brand-new*.

> "The Violet Fire is the most Powerful Activity of Divine Love,
> a Divine Gift of 'return to Holy Innocence'.
> The power to transmute leaves us with a brand-new start,
> with no karmic history or momentum.
> It is like being born again, over and over."
> ~ *Ascended and Free*

Every so often, in my meditations I persisted in asking, what does it mean, that Lilly told Spiritsong, 'I'm all brand new, the lightworkers created me'?

It means the Lightworkers created, by their longing, a format or thoughtform through which ones such as Lilly could express. Portions of the God Force that are 'all brand new', pristine in composition, can come and be a structure through which new geometries of existence may express. For your understanding, you could say she is angelic, of the angelics, angelic by nature or essence, in composition. And she could not come we might add to one who also did not bear this quality or frequency, as you have so often noted for others.

Of course I had questions! What about the seven years before she was with me? Like her mother, Lilly was a professional show girl, a champion in the show ring, and 'brood bitch'.

Always it was the same energy or 'entity', the same unit of energy, but the last time she was in hospital (being spayed) there was a bit of a switch or change over in the energies, in the geometries of her matrix. Some might call it a walk-in, as more of her higher self embodied, but it's somewhat more complex than that. For higher self is not an accurate description of her source energy. We do not speak of Source; we refer to the composite or collective from which she comes. The majority of it remains in spirit, but different portions of it are extended, you might say, into form, into matter for the purpose stated. Enough has been presented for now. We are of course, a part of your Brotherhood, Sisterhood, of Light and Love.

When Linda Rose, a friend who had stayed with the dogs when I was away, heard this she said, "Oh! That must be why the other dogs visit me (in her mind) as dogs, and Lilly comes as patterns of light geometries. I see her as an abstract dachshund because she is made of light and energy. The images I see of her are somewhat like a child's drawing, I know it's Lilly, but she's free flowing and everywhere."

> *She bears the tone of a song unsung,*
> *the dream of a world unborn.*
> *She is here to remind us to create in joy,*
> *to live each moment in wonder,*
> *surrender to a power unseen.*
> *She comes from inner space,*
> *a secret realm of unformed diamond light,*
> *a crystalline matrix of unstructured motion,*
> *a Holy Breath of waves in flow,*
> *a stream of silver, gold and dancing stars.*
> *Lilly is here to hold the Breath*
> *of Sacred Union with All That Is.*
> *Through an open heart she gives*
> *in every moment ~ with her most Holy Breath.*

~ ~ ~ ~ ~

Every week the dogs and I would visit their human 'granny' and I would leave them all alone together for half an hour. Lorna and Lilly and Candace. Time out for 'granny' to spoil them and pretend she had her own dogs again. On this occasion Lilly had jumped up on the table (via a chair) and tipped a box of birthday chocolates overboard. Lorna was the specialist in opening things. Chocolate is poison for dogs, and when I returned and saw them snuffling around a half empty box of chocolates, I knew immediately that I was going to lose them both. Candace remained sitting on her 'granny's lap, just the other side of an open sliding glass door into the garden.

I stayed with the dogs at the veterinary clinic for an hour or so, and suddenly felt the need to go home for a while. The two lady veterinarians seemed relieved. As I walked into the house the phone rang. Lorna had returned to Spirit. From somewhere deep inside I heard a tiny little voice say, *Lorna died. Oh no!* And I lay face down on the carpet, spontaneously raising my head to vocalize a beautiful, clear, high pitched, seemingly endless pure tone, not sad, not joyful, rather was it reminiscent of the song of a dolphin or the cry of a wolf. Every so often I paused to make sure this wasn't distressing Candace, and then continued. On and on. Normally, I cannot even tone a meaningful Ohm! And then I went back to the clinic, to be with Lilly as she was released from her physical body.

In sharing this experience with Marshall Golden Eagle Jack, he felt the tone I had released was a mixture of Lorna's joy and pain, and I heard;

It was a release, an opportunity to release the anguish of her lineage. Not trapped in form, so much as bound by Love. For they come in Service, bondage, as you know, to those whom they would free from their own iniquities. And Lorna jumped in joy at the opportunity to use the frequency of your unconditional loving compassion for all Life, to gain Freedom for her own ancestral lineage. Candace knew what was going on, she was simply holding the balance, the space, grounding you, we may say, to allow this to occur. It was a blessing as one small segment of Life's energies were requalified and returned to their original purity. The still small voice within is not accustomed to verbalizing physically, and that was the best it could do! ~ God bless, we are the Brotherhood of Love and Light.

Candace went to Spiritsong in a dream that night ~ in a glorious golden aura, surrounded by green fields and said, *Lorna knew Lilly was going, so she had to go first, because Lilly would not have known where to go or what to do.* She also said they could do more to help from 'the other side'.

When I tried to connect with Lorna my mind was filled with Light, brilliant pulsating Golden Light. Seemingly, she had returned directly to the Great Central Sun of All Creation. When I tried to connect with Lilly I heard, *she has returned to the Heart of the Mother.*

> *Lorna is deep within the Heart of Love.*
> *Lilly is deep within the Heart of the Mother.*
> *A double Ascension to Love and Light.*

And I remembered the time I had looked into Lorna's eyes and seen,

> *Sacred Geometry.*
> *Bright pools of darkness ~ each an orb,*
> *a universe of worlds untold.*
> *Her sweetness is my joy.*
> *Her love my gift from God Herself.*

"The first time I asked Lorna to visit me, there were big blue and white spirals spinning around inside my head and all around, a very electric blue with a dot in the center, many of them in geometric shapes. Lorna was communicating with those lightworkers who created Lilly, and the sacred geometric symbols." ~ *Linda Rose*

~ ~ ~ ~ ~

For the first year after Lorna's transition, I continued to experience her only as Light. Then she began to participate in our weekly Earth Healing meditations for the animals in her dog form. Working with the Katrina animals she helped bring in thousands to ascend through our Vortex of Love here in the Garden of Sananda.

This sort of work was not new to Lorna. In September 2001, I wrote Jamala; I am concerned about Lorna, she is so sad. She doesn't want to roam around the garden, she's not even interested when I open the 'fridge door, she just wants to stay in her chair. I have given her Rescue Remedy and anointed her paw pads with the essential oil of Harmony. I suppose she's 'working'?

He replied, "I checked in with Lorna ~ I'm sure you are aware that a lot of pets were stranded in apartments near the Trade Center. Owners were not allowed to go and rescue them. Lorna has been working with Heidi, Tiggy, Loreli and others with these trapped pets. Many have crossed over; some are still alive. Yesterday they started sending in owners with escorts to rescue them if possible. Lorna is very tired and very sad. We send her Energy and Light and support." I had not known about the trapped pets. Now I understand Lorna's grief and weariness.

I asked her if she might have a message of encouragement that I could share with everybody, and she gave me the thought that if we find it too hard to love everyone ~ *just love the mothers,* and to contemplate all a mother's love represents. Lorna continued to work with animals in disaster areas and our own meditation groups.

When she first came to us, I had the thought or 'knowing', that Lorna was a conduit for Kwan Yin, the Buddhist Goddess of Healing and Compassion. And when I was in the Holy Land, I was given a well-established Meditation and Healing group to share with them thoughts about the animal's role in this. I handed out a few photos of the dachshunds, people chose a picture, and we did a small meditation on how this animal might support or advise them. Many people had experiences that moved them to tears. One man held Lorna's picture at arm's length and proclaimed, through an interpreter, that he had just received a healing greater than any he had ever received from the group's founder. This produced much joyful laughter as Menorah was a spiritual healer of some renown!

I already knew that *Lilly was sent from the future, her purpose was to collect Lorna and bring her home. To ensure that she (Lorna) returned to Spirit to be where she was needed on time.* It was observed (by those in Spirit) that I was getting rather good at using a lot of natural or alternative healing methods to keep the dogs in form! Had Lilly not presented Lorna with the Doorway (the box of chocolates), Lorna would have remained, growing older and less able, and it was not intended for her to endure old age as Tiggy did.

I had also already been 'told' that *Lilly was never meant to become a part of your ongoing structure. Accept Lilly as a gift and blessing from Spirit. An experiment that was never intended to become an institution in your life. Enjoy the gift that was given. ~ God Bless, We Are That, Your Divine Self in form.* Lilly was with us for barely two years.

And so I made up a little story to tell others in a way that might be less upsetting than the bare essentials:

One day when she was nearly 16½ years old Lorna said to Lilly; *now then daughter, it's about time for me to go Home and I'm looking for a doorway.* Lorna was actually in very good health, so she added, *and I don't seem able to find one.* Lilly enthusiastically set about helping her mummy find a doorway, and when she found the box of chocolates, she called excitedly; *Mummy, mummy, I think I've found a doorway! But I don't know how to open it.* And Lorna said, *send it on down here daughter, I'll open it.* And Lilly tossed the box of chocolates off the table and jumped down beside her mother. And Lorna said, *now daughter, you are only nine years old, you do not have to follow me through this doorway.* And Lilly said, *yes, yes, mummy I do, I will never let you out of my sight again.*

"Where thou diest will I die,
and there will I be buried also."
~ Ruth verse 17

And I had the insight or thought, that Lilly is part of an angelic group working with those in transit. And to fully know how best to help, they must experience this for themselves. I felt her wonder (as in awe) at the love and care and concern that was offered to her little body at the veterinary clinic. The two lady vets working full time, they even closed the clinic saying, "we have a two-dachshund emergency."

Part of Lilly marveled at this outpouring of love, and part of her marveled at how attached humans are to the physical form, which is so temporary. Their lack of understanding in realizing that when it, the body, has completed its function to house the spirit, it is time to let it go, not try and force it to stay longer. She was both the observer and the experiencer. Knowing the *emotions* of receiving all this love and care Lilly had expanded the understanding and ability of her Group to assist others.

And I smiled to remember the time I had mindlessly asked the dogs, what *is* the meaning of Life? Lilly responded immediately;

Me. It's all about Me. I AM the meaning of Life!

"To respect yourself is to see the meaning of life."
~ *Peter Deunov (Beinso Douno)*

The Ascension of Candace

September 2007

Candace joined us at five years old and settled right in with her little dachshund relatives, Tiggy and Loreli, and her grandmother Lorna. I called them The Big Four. Candace arrived during one of our Animal Communication Playdays and wasted no time in telling one of the participants that she was Buddha's brother! Karen W had been doing very well, but at that point figured she may have 'lost it'! And asked me to ask Candace if she heard right. Never quite sure exactly how or if I can do such things, I only had to wonder and Candace responded immediately, seemingly somewhat indignant, *of course she heard right! I speak very clearly!* She had already indicated to Karen, that from her point of view, what Buddha did was not so smart or practical ~ to sit in one place under that Tree for so long. Hot and tired without food or sleep or water. Ever and always an empath, Candace felt compassion for this dedicated soul and said;

I was as the wind around his face.
for I was free form then
and did not Francis call the wind his brother?

"Smoke boasts to the sky, and Ashes to the earth,
that they are brothers to the fire."
~ Rabindranath Tagore

During our next Animal Communication Playday, Leslie brought four tiny orphan kittens she was fostering. Abandoned in a brown paper bag outside a local store, they were too young and vulnerable to be left alone all day. Leslie and kittens arrived early, and we let them out of their little blue Pet Taxi to experience the sun and the flowers and the grass. Enthusiastically, they tottered off in four different directions. Candace went wild with delight. Almost in a frenzy of concern, she tried to usher them back in their crate. She wanted to take care of them, and she wanted them all in one place. She just couldn't bring herself to pick them up in her mouth, so she poked them with her nose. Too small to resist, they were rolled over and over and prodded back into the crate, by which time the first one was out again. We helped Candace round them all up and left them on the front deck for morning 'class'. Candace sat at the glass front door watching them and crying gently to herself. Nobody was able to concentrate on anything!

At lunch time, the kittens were set loose in the kitchen and fed their bottles. Candace was a mess! Near delirious with joy and worry. And then we all went outside to a specially secluded area among the Pines that we call the Gnome Sanctuary to continue with our 'workshop'. Kittens, crate, dogs and all. The other three dogs barely acknowledged all this fuss about kittens. Exercises, meditation, or interspecies communication of any kind seemed impossible, as Candace scratched frantically at the Pet Taxi door, whining, and crying. Suddenly, in the same moment, we all 'got it' ~ we had to let Candace in with the kittens, and within my mind I heard her say;

Their cells are crying to my cells, and I must help them.

Leslie opened the door and Candace dived into the little crate full of kittens and mothered them to her heart's content. The little kittens, four white and one black, snuggled and climbed and nestled all over her, and Candace licked and licked and licked them, from top to bottom and back again. The most perfect demonstration of interspecies communication ~ through Love.

Empaths have the unique ability
to sense another's feelings or emotions,
which typically makes them extremely caring,
compassionate, and understanding.

Such a one was Candace.

The following week the kittens were brought back for a visit. Candace was just as pleased and excited to see them as she had been the first time, but now they were all a little bit more independent. This time they wouldn't allow themselves to be licked and rolled and herded back into their crate! Candace quickly adjusted to just keeping a general eye out for all four at the same time. The week after that, only two kittens came to visit, the two that Leslie adopted. The other kittens were also adopted together. When asked about the meaning of Motherhood, Candace replied;

It is a nurturing and caring responsibility. A mother is responsible for life regardless of its form. There were and are tribes who nurture any child in need, not just their own. I am of that Tribe. When there is a need my cells hear the call, every cell in my being responded to their cry for help at a cellular level.

For the next decade Candace's sweet sensitive nature continued to alert her to the needs of others. Her breeder said that the first time she had puppies, when they squeaked and cried, she sat in the middle and cried with them! But the next time she had babies, she happily fostered a couple of extras along with her own. And when I told her that Tiggy, who was nearly 18 years old, would soon be leaving, she looked at me in dismay and asked, *doesn't Tiggy love us anymore?*

Candace dearly loved her many human and animal friends and was of major importance during our meditation and Quantum Touch energy healing workshops. If anyone needed to lie on the massage table, Candace made it clear that she needed to be on the table too, and would lie pressed against them, her head usually resting on the area where they hurt most.

Friend Gerry, who placed a Peace Pole at the Pentagon, commented that she had never met a dog of such high consciousness, and was immediately aware that Candace was a great empath pooled into a vast system of knowledge, and that Candace was checking her out to see if she 'knew' this. Nearly twenty years later Dr. Gerry Eitner (PhD in ecopsychology) still recalls the encounter clearly saying, "I remember walking into the room; Candace was looking at me and I could immediately see/feel/connect with the ascending levels above her, all the way up to the Buddhic plane of awareness. My sense was of ten levels, and the Buddhic relationship was distinct. Candace was aware that I was connecting with her at these levels, and I remember you telling me afterwards that she said, *it was nice to be seen.* The whole experience blew me away. I've had many multidimensional experiences with people and animals, but this was extreme, distinct, immediate, and very memorable."

The thought for me when looking into Candace's eyes was ~ *to think that I hold within my arms one who knew Buddha, who brought him comfort, as she comforts me. How blessed I am.*

~ ~ ~ ~ ~

Candace seemed to be doing alright after Lorna and Lilly left us, but she went into great sadness when the carpet went, and with it all the smells and memories of her beloved little companions. But then, her new friends, Bella the Great Dane and five Siamese cats invited us for supper and time out by the big fire in their lovely octagonal home. Bella and her family gently welcomed Candace into their own living space, and a week or so later, we were invited back.

I mentioned to Bella's human that Bella's big bark had scared Candace, so Ingrid said she would speak to Bella about that ~ and on our next visit, Bella came up to the car and quietly put her whole head inside to welcome her little friend back. Her head was bigger than all of Candace! Candace gently wagged her tail and seemingly had no more sadness.

When the time came that I visited Bella's home without Candace, I didn't see Bella. Where is she? "She's gone to your car," said Miles, Bella's other human, "she's looking for Candace."

Several years earlier, Ingrid had found Bella standing in the middle of a country road, so she opened the car door and Bella climbed in. No-one in the area had ever seen her before. In a meditative state, I asked about this, where had she come from? And heard, *she is essence from the Heart of the Great Central Sun*. And I saw the image of a Master reach forth his arm and with outstretched fingers take a pinch of this essence, and with a flick of his fingers, throw it ~ to land in the form of Bella, right where Ingrid was on a trajectory or angle of movement to connect with it. And now, when thinking about Bella and her gentle friendship with sweet Candace, I had the thought (from Bella); *I know her essence well*, and seemingly as a reflection, a sort of far-off memory;

Candace got caught in the rifts along the River of Life. But now she is free. All the little ones who come to Sananda are free (to return to essence). Mostly, they are free before they come, it is as though they have a short while of rest and repose in gentleness and safety, that they may remember their earthly lives in joy.

Now that she was an 'only dog', Candace loved to sleep in her little bed on the back doorstep surrounded by the brightly blooming portulaca, where she could keep an eye on me while I was doing gardening things. Suddenly I heard her barking, but it was a bark like none other I had ever heard ~ and Candace was a grand little barker! Every time someone came to the door, she could sense or 'see' what was in their energy fields and if she didn't like it, she didn't want them in or anywhere near her house! But this bark was totally different, this was more like an alert, a gentle but demanding; *Attention everybody! Listen! Look! Behold!*

Candace was standing up, looking out across the paddock. I followed her gaze, and saw three people, several dogs, a horse ~ and a new baby! Standing up! The grey mare has delivered her child! At midday, in three and a half minutes flat! Standing on her kitchen doorstep, Candace was gently wagging her tail and offering sweet welcome woofs! There are two fences and quite a bit of garden between us all, how could she see so far? She was asleep! How did she know? I must ask her to put in words her feelings, her knowing ~ my thoughts were intercepted;

*All Life should be welcomed.
It is a big decision for Life to enter form,
and it should be honored.*

Candace is such a good little dog. I told Spiritsong the hot weather made her pant; Spiritsong said the hot weather made her pant too.

One day when we were having a little sit down together, I reminded Candace that Loreli is Healing the Planet (according to Loreli that is), and has 'gone Galactic'. And Tiggy is hanging out with the Fairies and is now in charge of all the Dragonflies. And Lorna is deep within the Heart of Love, and her daughter Lilly is deep within the Heart of the Mother (Lorna), and you Candace ~ are the focal point for all this Power and Glory. They will help you if you want! Candace wagged her tail and bounced around a bit. And surely, I thought, surely Buddha himself will help the little dog who called him her Brother, and in her great compassion for one who sat so long beneath a Tree, wafted a cool and loving breeze around him. Candace had given us this story on the first day she arrived at Sananda so long ago, at five years old. Now I ask her, Candace, how would you like us to think of you? *I AM Candace of Sananda!* And I smiled greatly to myself. Yesterday, I had been thinking she should be called Candace of Sananda, but I had left out the I AM.

~ ~ ~ ~ ~

Time passed, and at nearly 15 years old, Candace just wasn't having fun anymore. Nothing specific, just acute discomfort (screams) if one touched or picked her up wrong, to such an extent that she no longer enjoyed being cuddled or snuggled beside me in the recliner, although she still slept on my bed. A few months earlier the vet reported that her eyes were in great shape, but now she was walking through the middle of plants and bushes, seemingly not seeing them. At other times, she would be happily trotting across the lawn and come to a sudden crashing halt, as though she had run into a brick wall. And there were various other little upsets ~ disorienting for her and distressing for me.

I phoned our good friend Melissa to tell her the veterinarian would come in the morning, and although it was late evening and Melissa must arise at 5 am, she came immediately to help ease the mind and body of her dear canine friend. Candace was anointed with essential oils and all the other healing care Melissa offers. Curled up in her little cuddler bed, in her own gentle way, I could tell by her eyes how glad she was to see her human friend. Candace relaxed deeply and slept well that night. She was snug in her little cuddler bed beside me when the veterinarian came next morning.

In the evening, Neil and her other friends gathered to help prepare her Space of Love beside all the other little dachshunds at the edge of the pine trees. Wrapped in a pretty cotton cloth, I laid her on a blanket of soft sweet smelling dried grass clippings. Renee picked all the prettiest flowers in the garden, and we layered her with the huge bouquet, and more grass clippings, fine earth and pine needles. We placed a beautiful clump of pale blue Celestite crystal on top and circled it with lots of fresh white sage. So pretty it was. Honoring her life in form, with gratitude for all she had shared with us, then and now. Helping others resolve the grief they experienced with their own beloved animals.

Cindy played Amazing Grace on her little tin whistle, Melissa played her Native American flute, Ingrid sang, chanting a profound Native American blessing. And we heard the words, *finally all those decisions are over.* And I had a beautiful vision of Candace, as one who had been at the bottom of an ocean, headed straight up to the surface where she burst with great joy into the Light and was greeted by all her little friends, and a host of others standing round about.

Others had similar visions of her being greeted by her 'pack'. Jim expressed joy *in celebration of her ascension into the realms of Light from which she came.* And had an image *of all those little critters racing around. Their light bodies appeared 'Tinker Bell' size, nothing but light energy, and their joy at the arrival of one of their own was extreme. They were celebrating and taking 'time off' from their normal activities to welcome Candace home.* And Candace murmured, *free at last!*

I emailed those of her friends who could not be present; "Candace had a joyous Celebration of Life Ceremony and is flying high in the Sun of Forever ~ with Tiggy and Loreli and Lorna and Lilly and All."

The next day, Melissa phoned to say she had received a vision of Candace walking over a little rainbow bridge, with her own cat Poncho. And on the other side, was a beautiful little path with a stream on one side and flowers on the other, and trees, and everything so green and lovely, and Candace and Poncho simply dispersed into waves of energy which appeared as gentle flowing movement in the flowers and water. *That's how I knew where they were,* said Melissa. They expanded vibrationally in all directions until they simply were no more. They had merged to become one with all of Nature.

"I believe in God, only I spell it Nature." ~ *Frank Lloyd Wright*

Oneness through Nature ~ Ascension.

Spiritsong dreamed that Candace was met by a host of friends and others, supervised by a small long-haired Pomeranian who said; *This is my first assignment, I hope I do it right!* And a voice from the back (Loreli for sure) said; *A little less talking might be nice!* And Candace indicated to Spiritsong also, that she was so very glad to be free of that body. *Every day it was one more thing.* Candace also told her the reason she would stand staring at the walls (a new thing in the last few days, and different from getting stuck in the flowers or under a chair); *I was looking for the portal, and I couldn't find it.*

A few weeks later, when friends were staying overnight, the conversation turned to a young man who kept walking into things because he could see through them, and I wondered if that was what happened to Candace with the bushes and flowers, and the 'invisible' obstacles? It wasn't that her eyesight had failed, it was more that she was seeing into a different dimensional reality (as Tiggy had already explained to us in *The Ascension of Heidi*), especially when she was outdoors in Nature.

It was November before Melissa's next visit. She had just buried another cat, the one that slept on her bed. Quietly she said, "I did *everything* we did for Candace." She searched for flowers. "I even found the rose. One rose! And some sage." The rose was important to her because Candace had a rose. "And I covered the earth back over him with my hands, just as Neil did. I did everything we did for Candace!"

We lit a candle and some sage, and played soft music. Melissa sat on a chair, and I stood behind her offering Quantum-Touch (energy healing) through her shoulders. In her mind, she saw the cat go through an Orb of Light, and Candace was there to encourage him. *It's easy,* said Candace, gently waving her tail for the cat to follow, but to Melissa who also tried to follow she said, *you can't come in!* But she let Melissa peek through a window *because you came to visit me the night before I went.* Candace had by far the most magnificent, feathered tail of all the dachshunds.

~ ~ ~ ~ ~

Time went by and one fine summer day, when I was sitting between the pine trees, I became centered and silent, and aware of a small cooling breeze. A breeze! A Candace specialty! In the beginning, when Candace first left us, I would call on her for help in the garden. I would ask her for rain ~ for more rain, or less rain, for less wind, for cloud cover ~ and it always happened! When telling a friend about this, she said; "Oh! Candace is an Air Spirit! She's a Sylph!"

Once again, I apologized to Candace, for not letting her go sooner.

It's alright, she said, *I didn't really want to go any earlier. I came to be with a pack. Now I am free form. I really like being free form. But I can visit if I want to ~ in consciousness. I can think myself wherever I want to be. Do I have a job? Does the air have a job?! I AM. I AM part of Beauty and Silence and Motion, and I AM in all things.*

And then it seemed that a greater or more encompassing part of her took over, and I heard;

Candace can be and is, everywhere present. Call upon her when in need for she is far more than Candace. She is an emanation of God's Breath Herself. You came to share this knowledge, these teachings, and the time is now. Who are we? We are yourselves. Nature combined. For you too are an emanation of God's Holy Breath, the Wave ~ and the particles, you might say, are what some call the Elementals, and which we say are expressions of Nature playing, communicating with Herself.

The Fairies and the Gnomes, the Elves and the Sprites. All is One. And when your dogs, your beloved pets depart and people say, 'a part of me has gone with them', how truly they speak! But gone where? Gone only from sight and touch and feel, the physical senses. In Spirit they are ever present, here, there and forever.

Candace is with you, but not in form, she is freedom expressed in feeling tones. She has consciousness, she is essence, pure essence of Divine Love that goes where it desires and goes where it can make a difference to those who know, who recognize the frequency of her blessing. You may call this frequency Candace if you wish, but she too has a spirit name ~ just ask. Ask and it shall be given. Now quiet time.

So we had a little talk and I asked her what is she called now? And I heard, *She'anana ~ Sheanana.* So beautiful! So gentle.

"Try to hear the name the Holy Ones have for things.
People name everything according to the number of legs they have.
The Holy Ones name them according to what they have inside." ~ *Rumi*

Later still, when I was working in the garden, outside the kitchen door where Candace loved to sit and I tend to think of her whenever I am in this area, clearly within my mind I heard a sweet soft voice I knew as Candace say, *I'm here!* Next day, it poured with rain. Idiotically I thought, oh dear! I hope Candace is alright! I hope she has somewhere she can go to keep dry! And I heard her say, *I AM the rain!*

"I love to think of Nature as an unlimited broadcasting station
through which God speaks to us every hour
if we will but listen."
~ *George Washington Carver*

Linda Rose emailed; "Candace is still part of my life, every day. At night she flickers on my ceiling as geometric patternings of Light with a Candace shape, it's been there ever since I first moved into my apartment a year after I visited you, and got to love the Garden of Sananda and all its wonderful beings."

"Let us contemplate the nature of Light ~ individual photons of Light operate beyond time and space. In this Oneness Consciousness, if one photon is here and another photon is there, then both photons know they are both here and there ~ and further, with all the infinite other photons in Universal Light, they are collectively everywhere present ~ with each photon knowing I AM here, there and I AM everywhere present!" ~ *Ascended and Free*

~ ~ ~ ~ ~

September 2020, school shut down. Melissa does not have a good internet connection at her home, so she was teaching her music classes for the county school here at Sananda. Although it is thirteen years since Candace returned to Spirit, I am ever eager to hear more from the little dachshunds and suggested that she re-connect with Candace and ask if perhaps Candace had seen her (Melissa's) own kitties who recently returned to Spirit ~ and while she was at it, to ask Candace if she really knew Saint Francis of Assisi, whose image and statues are all over the house and garden.

Melissa felt that she had a stronger connection to Spirit when she was here at Sananda but agreed to try that evening, to ask Candace if she could hear her there, in her own home. However, Melissa had trouble remembering, saying or even thinking the words 'Saint Francis of Assisi'! Candace came through promptly, clearly, and humorously, saying, *you mean does Saint Francis of Assisi know ME!*

I asked Francis about this ~ does he really know Candace?!

He responded, *Of course! She is one of the great Devas.*

> "The Devic Kingdoms
> are in Service to the planet and to all Life."
> ~ *John Payne channeling Omni*

And I remembered dear friend and Animal Communicator Barb Janelle looking into Candace's eyes and remarking,

> "Huge pools of quiet knowledge,
> really remarkable, very profound.
> Not only in Service to Humanity
> but to the entire planet."

The Ascension of Olivia

March 2008

Olivia and her mother Primrose have arrived! Since Candace left, I have been without a dog all winter and wasn't quite sure if I wanted these two. And here they are. Untamed, untrained little wildlings! The same lineage as the others but kennel raised, never been shown, and with no social skills whatsoever! Very tiny, and of course, adorable.

Darling Olivia, the little adventuress, how fast she could run! Off she went, flying out of the door with invisible streamers of *explore explore explore* trailing behind her. No matter how hard I had tried to call her Olivia, it usually came out as Lilly, even though Lilly and her mother Lorna had been gone for nearly four years. I always felt, at nine years old, that Lilly had not had her fair share of being at Sananda.

Not long after their arrival, I had to go out of state to give a pre-arranged Paneurhythmy workshop so they, Olivia and her mum, had a wonderful week up the road and round the corner with Neil and Chuck. Every day Neil carried them, one under each arm, to their outside pen where they were visited by the neighbor's little blue eyed blond three-year-old human angel. Eventually, he could just open the 'gate', and with shining eyes and flapping ears they would go racing back to their little beds and bowls and blankets in the kitchen.

And then I returned. They were so excited to come back to a place they knew ~ and were definitely a little more sedate than when they left. Perhaps they thought I had given them away and they should try and behave a bit. Anyway, they went flying around the outside of the house and in through the back door to re-discover all their assorted toys and treasures. And in the evening, Olivia curled herself in a tiny little ball on my lap in the big recliner with Primrose stuffed at our side. Olivia had only three days left to play in her own garden.

One day, after her early morning journey of discovery ~ she came joyfully racing back over the dew drenched grass and collapsed at my feet. I rushed her to the vet, although I knew within my heart that she was leaving us. The next day the veterinary clinic phoned to say she could come home that evening, but that was not to be ~ by the time I arrived Olivia was on life support. I held her tightly as she was given help in releasing from her little body. She was only two years old and with us for less than a month.

Spiritsong and I talked that night, but it seemed she had other things on her mind, and I wasn't sure how much of Olivia's passing had registered. And yet, that night she dreamed ~ a mist wavered in front of me, and a soft voice from within said;

Tell Sananjaleen not to mourn my departure. I was in no pain. It went as planned and I had ascended prior to the last day, only the shell remained. Sananjaleen was right to call me Lilly, all brand new, for I am the essence of Lilly. There was a final cleansing of the vortex known as Sananda that needed to be completed, I volunteered and was happy to do so. Primrose will handle anything that surfaces, she is to act as an anchor. Know again, that I suffered no pain, I had already left. Now I must move forward. Keep the white light around everyone, contact is but a tail wag away.

The mist faded and floated away, and I (Spiritsong) gasped to see Red Cloud (Oglala Lakota Chief), move forward with leaves of Mullein. He too said;

Keep the white light, the purple flame around you at all times. There are experiments taking place now to poison the blood supply of one and all, but fear not, we will protect. The good will always prevail, although it may not seem so in the short term. Take Mullein leaves, a quart of tea, and sip on it throughout the day, it will purify the blood. Eat only things growing close to home. Be careful of canned goods and the water you drink. Be wise. We shall return ~ in the meantime, stay away from crowds. This was given in 2008.

~ ~ ~ ~ ~

I wished that Olivia could have had more time to rush through the house with little stuffed bunnies in her mouth, dig up more cat poop, shred more Kleenex, make more puddles, bark at more horses, sniff more flowers and shred more organic dried sweet potato chews. But she made it to the Garden of Sananda to complete her Ascension, and whatever it was that Lilly did not have the opportunity to finish. And she did so, seemingly in the joy of knowing that her mission was accomplished.

> "I slept and dreamt that life was joy.
> I woke and saw that life was service.
> I acted and beheld ~ service was joy."
> ~ Rabindranath Tagore

"Joy is the happiness that doesn't depend upon what happens." ~ Anon

And even before Spiritsong's dream, I knew:

> *Olivia was essence unformed.*
> *A passing breeze that served completion*
> *for a previous time.*

The Ascension of Primrose

March 18, 2012

Petite and adorable, Primrose was seven years old when she and her daughter Olivia arrived. Untrained and seemingly untrainable little wildlings! They were still sleeping in their kitchen pen at night when Olivia left us. Primrose had never been alone before, so come nightfall, I carried her down the hallway and placed her on my bed. *No way!* She launched herself into space and went racing back to the safety of her own little bed and blankie. Apparently that was not a happy choice, and thereafter she was very willing to sleep with me.

Primrose brought us great joy and enchantment. She did such adorable things. She was always so full of fun. Every time I came home, she would grab one of her little beds by the rim, prancing and dancing around the room as she tossed the thing over her shoulder and vandalized all her squeaky toys. She loved being in the garden and although I had long taken down the inside pen, I still popped her in the outside one when I couldn't watch her all the time. She disapproved quite heartily.

Primrose reminded me very much of Loreli. In fact, it often seemed that it was Loreli looking at me through her eyes, and because there were no other little dachshunds to teach her what she needed to know, I figured there was an agreement, and that Loreli had come to show her the routine. Pretty soon after her arrival, Primrose went to Spiritsong in a dream and told her that she had come *to gather up all the messages*. She had to *collect the messages*. We had no idea what that meant, but she did go all over the garden, very busily, seemingly seeking and searching. Was she checking on messages left by the other dachshunds? Like seeds they had sewn. There was something I couldn't quite grasp.

And then I read, that wherever we walk, wherever we go, we leave an imprint of our DNA upon the land, and I understood *that the land holds the imprint or patterning of that which has been. Each seed or message was a code, a 'light code', a sacred geometry of information or instructions, inactive until something brings them to life,* and Primrose, her presence or frequency was the catalyst, the activation necessary for their release into her being or awareness of these codes or messages. And I heard, *individual electronic patterns of light, unique geometric patternings, stamped or imprinted with her own.* What she did with them was a mystery! Maybe she didn't do anything with them, maybe she simply enabled their release, the release of information, into the atmosphere, where it would be available as needed.

A decade later, in the 2023 Animal Welfare Institute fall magazine, I read that analysis of genetic material (DNA) shed by animals' footprints into their environment (e-DNA) was being used to track and identify polar bear populations! Samples of the upper layer of snow from their footprints were thawed and filtered to capture DNA in the form of epidermal cells shed by their paw pads. Results provided evidence that e-DNA collected from footprints could be used to identify individual bears. Primrose, it seems, was way ahead of the researchers!

Meanwhile, Spiritsong had a second dream where Primrose told her; my companion cleared out the darkness that had been left by someone. *I'm gathering my messages; I have to get them right you know! We both volunteered for our missions.* Was 'her companion' her daughter Olivia? The veterinarian had never diagnosed why she died so abruptly. The symptoms were poison, but there was no proof of this. Had she in fact absorbed and transmuted a darkness?

And then, little Schatzi came to live with us. Son of Lilly, and grandson of Lorna, Schatzi had often been to visit in the past and he and Primrose quickly became inseparable. I called him her Prince Charming, but she told good friend and neighbor Laurie he was *not* her Prince Charming. He was her surrogate puppy! Either way, he took good care of her, and she seemed forever happy and filled with Joy and Adventure.

Primrose also demonstrated profound awareness. Friend Ingrid arrived with Bella the Great Dane. Although it was very hot, the sun was well shaded by clouds, and after a while of being outside, we put Bella in Ingrid's station wagon under the trees and took a quick visit indoors. Schatzi came inside with us, and I was aware that Primrose had remained outside. Pretty soon I heard intense barking. Primrose was sitting under the Pine tree just outside the front door uttering short sharp barks. As soon as I went to the door and looked out at her, she stopped barking and turned her head to point at Ingrid's car which was now in *full sun*. I hurried back to tell Ingrid and Primrose started barking again. As soon as Ingrid appeared at the door, she stopped barking and repeated the head turn of 90 degrees pointing her nose towards the car. As soon as Ingrid touched the car door handle Primrose got up and came inside.

> I am holding Primrose in my arms and wondering,
> who she really is ~ where does she really come from?
> Primrose is Love embodied.
> Does anything else really matter?

Primrose also had a grand sense of humor. My notes say: It is January, 9 degrees, and the UPS man has arrived in his shorts. Big excitement for the dogs. Primrose came in with a frozen mouse in her mouth. Prying a frozen mouse out of her mouth with gloves on is not easy, but not quite as unpleasant as battling for ownership of a big fat soft squashy fresh kill, which I had to do five times this fall. That was so awful, the mouse was so soft and squashy, and I had to get a grip and pull so hard, I was afraid it might burst. At first, Primrose fought back fiercely, teeth and eyes flashing. Now she just hangs on. I always give her a little dog cookie in return for letting me have mouse. Primrose Version:

Such a lovely day. The man with Boxes arrived again and Shatzi and I sent him running back to his truck. Schatzi followed the box into the house, but I went scout about. I followed Nose and found a lovely little frozen mouse, buried near Best Cat Poop Place. Funny how we like the same things, She and Me. She gets all excited when she sees me headed towards the house. Saying things like; 'Wait. Wait. Give it to me, give it to me'. Such a fuss. She wants it so much, I don't know why she doesn't follow her own Nose. Anyway, I let her have it. She always gives me something in return. Something less than half the size of my eyeball though. But I can always find another mouse.

I have trained Schatzi to let Her know when I want to come back in the house. He is always pleased to see me and takes good care of Chew Bones while I am out. 'Here they are Princess', he says, and steps back so I can be with them again. Sometimes I let him chew one of them. He doesn't hurt them, I'm the one who makes them smaller and smaller until they just disappear into me forever. I've trained Her well too, she moves our furry blanket around so it's always in the sun. And another one in front of the fire. Life is good.

Primrose was also big into Responsibility and Motherhood. She was all curled up in preparation for a boring evening when three six-week-old baby Norfolk puppies arrived for four days. Primrose was in ecstasy ~ inside the kitchen pen with them and all their beds and blankets and toys and diaper pads, and they are in ecstasy with her. And their breeder is thrilled to have Primrose discipline them! Needless to say, she barely slept all night, and was up and off my bed at the smallest whimper from the kitchen. She feels very responsible. On Mother's Day, I asked, from her perspective, how did she view this day?

Mother's Love is sacred, for it is the birth of Life, the allowance of Life to permeate where Life was not. Life waits in silence to be born. Living in Love until the day it leaves the experience and flows, returns from whence it came. And though the experience may be painful or disgraced, the Love remains, for it is the essence of Life, never diminished or destroyed, only hidden or suppressed. Love is ever. Seek Love in all Life ~ for it is ever present.

Primrose, it seemed, was also some kind of medical intuitive. My notes say: Primrose has gone mad trying to eat all the golden dandelions in sight. I hurried inside to google 'dogs eating dandelions'. The information was such that I wondered if perhaps I also should get down on all fours and follow her lead. My notes also read; 'Today Primrose ate a stink bug. It was hard work'.

Primrose was also a heart specialist! Someone came for a Quantum-Touch (energy healing) session, which turned out to be pretty much an expansion in consciousness. Brenda commented that the different colors she was seeing in her mind had condensed and formed into a little dachshund face that was smiling right into her own! Schatzi always came into the healing room when people came, and usually went under the bed, but now Primrose has joined us too ~ and hangs out in full view.

When Brenda returned for her second QT session both dogs followed us into the healing room, and for the first time Schatzi did not go under the bed. They both lay down and I forgot about them. After about twenty minutes, I was sitting on the high stool with my hands held lightly around Brenda's head when Primrose stepped forward, stood up on her hind legs, paws on my knee, and gazed deeply into my eyes. "She wants me to tell you something", I told Brenda, "But I don't know what. See if you can figure it out".

Pretty soon Brenda had tears rolling down her face. She was remembering a miniature long-haired dachshund they had 38 years ago. The family had to move, and the next house would not allow dogs, so they left Bugsy with the new owner of their old home. Originally, they had saved Bugsy from severe neglect and nursed her back to health. Thanks to Primrose, Brenda was able to bring this hidden trauma to the surface and send Bugsy love and gratitude. She felt a great sense of relief from sadness and pressure.

Primrose also had a need for adventure! Looking out of the kitchen window I saw a dozen or so vultures sitting on the far paddock fence. I knew they 'had something' as I had seen them down on the grass earlier. But now, already halfway across the paddock, tiny little Primrose was headed out towards them. Pausing every few steps to take a good look and sniff the air, she was headed for their kill, wherever it was. So tiny she was. So big the birds. I must go out and bring her home, but first, I turned to get my camera. Only a few seconds and I was out the door ~ just in time to see Primrose racing back towards the house! So fast she ran! But not in terror, there seemed to be a joyful air of *WHOA!!!* around her as she ran. What changed her mind? One of the vultures stood up on the fence and stretched out its wings! By the time Primrose was back in the garden she was laughing! Laughing and panting and ready for the next adventure.

The previous week the vultures had been out there, but their 'something' was near the garden fence and Primrose had slipped in when they were out and about and brought a neck home. Somebody's boney hairless neck. The next day, I silently asked Primrose if she had any comments regarding yesterday. Somewhat indignantly, she retorted, *they need to learn to share!*

Primrose and Schatzi loved to spend time at their other home up the road with Laurie and her two little dogs and all their toys. On 'movie nights', Laurie would set all these toys, stashed in one of the little dog beds, in the middle of the floor waiting for her, and Primrose would get them all out and squeak them to death, and very often, she would put them all back! Tucking and poking them into the dog bed with her nose, just like they were her little puppies. Then she joined us on the couch where she would get her '$40-dollar massage'. I had seen at the dog shows that these 'massages' were $40 for 20 minutes or so. Laurie would 'massage' her anyway! She and Primrose adored each other, and much to her mystification, Primrose came quite frequently into her dreams, usually prefixed by the words, *we interrupt this sleep to bring you a message from Primrose!* Or on her morning meditational walks, *we interrupt this walk for another transmission from Primrose!* Laurie never got over it!

"How weird is this, that I would dream a dog was talking to me? *And break into the middle of another dream! Saying things like, I want you to listen to this, I want you to know this.* And she (Primrose) was smiling! She wants everyone to understand that she wants to have fun. And then, when I'm just walking along minding my own business, all of a sudden I hear, *we interrupt this blessing counting to deliver an important message to you from Primrose!* Literally out of the blue!" Sometimes in her dream, Primrose replayed a daytime incident, showing, giving or telling the true or deeper meaning of an event.

At that time, I was giving a lot of Quantum-Touch (energy healing) workshops. One of the suggestions for increasing the energy flowing through our hands was to think happy thoughts. The first time Laurie did this, silently asking; *What can I think of to make me smile, to make me joyful, to make me laugh,* and in her mind she heard, *open your eyes.* And there was Primrose, sitting directly opposite her on the white couch, offering eye contact. Primrose was not supposed to be on this white couch, she hopped up and down again, just for that purpose, she knew Laurie's need and she responded. And for every workshop thereafter, whatever room Laurie was in, she only had to think or wonder 'what would make me smile' ~ and Primrose would always appear, directly in front of her.

And then we had an Animal Communication workshop or playday. Five or six of us sitting in a circle on the floor with the Medicine Cards spread out in front of us. These are tarot cards, each depicting a picture of a north American animal. I would start the class with each person drawing a card and asking their particular animal how it could help them. Primrose and Schatzi were asleep, one each side of me, and I was just explaining that there were four blank cards, in which case one could draw another card or decide on an animal of choice. All in the same moment ~ I was still in the middle of explaining this, when Primrose arose, walked through the middle of the cards towards Laurie who was holding up a blank card ~ and deliberately sat down in front of her!

Next morning Laurie reported; "Yes, I would definitely say that Primrose asserted herself as to who would be my guide. She obviously wanted to make it known that she was the only one to be *my* teacher, not some other animal on a tarot card. In between wakefulness and falling asleep last night she came to me with one simple thought statement; *Well, of course it is me who is your guide. Who else would it be?*"

So! Primrose is out and about in Laurie's dreams when I think she's asleep on my bed! What else might she be doing one wonders?! I was beginning to feel a bit left out! Holding her in my arms as we sat in the recliner I asked what Primrose might share with me.

Primrose is an activator. She has come to activate you. The time is now, to share and tell. She is the wrap up module you might say. She will bring together all the events of the past. The experiences and transmissions, the 'messages' as you call them, that others may know and benefit from and be themselves activated. Like Loreli, Primrose enjoys her body, her task in dog form, she delights in the mystery she creates. She likes to think of herself as a little magician, a master magician!

Primrose was also extremely observant. Knowing how much she enjoyed disemboweling and de-squeaking the toys, Laurie arrived one day with a small foam frisbee. "She won't know what to do with that," I said. Laurie ignored me, smiled at Primrose, tossed it across the room and said, go fetch! Primrose immediately jumped down from the couch, trotted over to the frisbee, picked it up, took it to Laurie, and returned to the couch. And I recalled that once, on one of our little walks, she had seen another dog play frisbee!

Laurie also noted; "She sits up so prettily for a treat. She started doing that on her own after watching Sandy (one of Laurie's little dogs)!

No one taught her, it was purely from observation. And I was so proud of her coming in all by herself through the doggie door! She followed the other three dogs. It gives me goosebumps thinking about what else she watches, observes, and absorbs."

> "I see in Primrose, through her eyes,
> and vibrating through her whole being
> an amazing spark of Light!
> She is truly an angelic being." ~ *Crystal*

~ ~ ~ ~ ~

Early one March morning Primrose awoke throwing up. Snug in her little cuddler bed I carried her to the veterinary clinic every day for three days. On the third day I awoke with the thought, *supposing she needs to be out of here by the Equinox*. Yes, said the veterinarian, who could only assume it was abdominal cancer, Primrose has work to do elsewhere. She was only ten years old ~ her eyes so bright and beautiful.

That evening her friends gathered for the *Earthing of Primrose* as we laid yet another little Dachshund to rest beneath the Pines of Sananda. I picked all the finest daffodils in the garden and Neil created a sacred space for the little cloth wrapped bundle amongst the soft, sweet smelling dried grass clippings. Melissa, who had cried all the way here, added lots of small blue and yellow anemone blanda, the windflowers that were carpeting the land. Laurie added her favorite little squeaky bear, and also cried all the way through ~ and we all so greatly admired the way Neil was arranging the daffodils that he looked up through his own tears, to tell us that he had just completed a Flower Arranging Course at the National Cathedral!

Just a few feet away, the three horses stood by the fence watching closely and gently nickering, and as we started to sprinkle the earth over the little bundle that held her body, one of them stepped forward, leaned over the fence and neighed loudly ~ seemingly honoring their little friend by trumpeting the last Taps. Primrose loved to coyly venture a little way into their field and bark at them. They knew each other well. Melissa played gently on her native American flute.

Everyone had close family members, dogs included, who had recently died or might go at any moment. Primrose provided a Space of Love for all to cry together. I sprinkled the essential oil of Joy upon us all, for that is what she was. The Veterinary clinic sent a nice card, signed by the two vets and all the technicians and receptionists, one of whom wrote; "Primrose was such a dear little cat!"

That night, as I gazed at the sunset and wondered where was she? Where did Primrose go? I heard; *she is beyond the Sun ~ beyond the sun that you see*. And I sensed the words *Love Beings, Love Beings*, and I felt motion, movement, and I just couldn't grasp who or what it was.

Primrose is Essence. What did we tell you?
Primrose is Love embodied, Cosmic Essence in form.
And I was overwhelmed by the Power of Love.

Eventually I began to comprehend the Love Beings as a Forcefield. And my attention was drawn to the great Archangel Sandalphon, sometimes described as the 'Unified Field'. Sandalphon! The Unified Field! *That's what the Love Beings are!* The Ones who greeted Primrose! They re-arranged themselves to create a portal or opening allowing her to flow back to Source. And I had a vision of Primrose as the tiniest dot wonderingly entering this *vastness*. The awesomeness, the bravery of this tiniest of specks entering into this vastness was so overwhelming that I had to arise and gather some Kleenex. And I heard, *returning to Love is ... such a supremely profound experience* that I didn't remember anything else.

"True Love is so powerful that if you made contact with it,
you could hardly support its vibrations, and just a few seconds
would be enough for you to remember for all eternity."
~ *Peter Deunov (Beinso Douno)*

The Love Beings opened to receive her, welcoming her Home into their Cosmic Forcefield of Divine Love ~ and I realized that every time I think of Primrose, I receive a blessing from the Love Beings. It is as though the heavens open and a cascading waterfall of Divine Love flows down, through, around, and upon me. Did I just realize this? Or am I intending and creating it?

When you, or anyone else, think of Primrose with Love, this Love flows to and through her essence enhancing the Whole, the One. Not the template through which she came, for she has disconnected from that (her little earthly body), but others (Beings of Light) may use it if required. But it is the template through which their expression would flow, not her essence. Love needs no form in which to be. Love needs only a focus through which to express, to show Love's Light ~ and Light loves all.

> "Love is the only reality,
> it is the ultimate truth
> that lies at the heart of Creation."
> ~ Rabindranath Tagore

Was it Sandalphon who welcomed Primrose home? *It was.* So in a way, Primrose was an emanation of Sandalphon? *She was. You could say that.*

> "Love Beams from the Sun is what you are,
> as Flame and its Radiance,
> and then you blend with the Cosmic Light."
> ~ Ascended and Free

> "Primrose transitioned from embodied consciousness
> into Solar Consciousness. Particle-function life
> returning to a wave-function State of Consciousness."
> ~ adapted from Ascended and Free

The Ascension of Schatzi

May 3, 2012

Schatzi was destined for life in the Show Ring but when he was only 18 months old it was discovered that he had a heart murmur. This was not expected to bother him until he was about nine years old, so he was offered to me as a pet, but I already had three little daxies, including his mother Lilly, and grandmother Lorna, and really didn't want a fourth. Friend Helga was thrilled to accept him.

However, when he was only four years old Schatzi had a major heart crisis. He was in surgery for five hours and not expected to live more than another three months. But he did! They called him the Miracle Dog. Helga wrote, "The entire hospital was rooting and praying for him and carried him around like a baby. When he came home, it was touch and go for a week and I was awake most nights with him in my arms scared he might die. He is the only bright beam in my life, and we need each other. The doctor and nurses from the hospital called every other day to see how he was, they truly think he is a miracle." Schatzi continued to take care of his beloved person for the next seven years. She called him her savior.

I was away when Helga died. The clairvoyant friend I was staying with saw my distress and said, *Helga is alright, Schatzi escorted her to the other side!* I couldn't imagine how he did this, but I still share the information ~ that Schatzi is available as an escort and can be called upon to escort both humans and animals to the 'other side'.

And so, Schatzi came to live with Primrose and me and we were very happy to have him. His gentle love and caring ways continued to bring comfort and joy to all who held him to their hearts. One day when I was reading about an oil spill in Florida and how the beautiful beaches were littered with dead dolphins, I spontaneously burst into tears. Immediately I felt Schatzi's little nose brush my foot. And then he was in my arms, staring into my eyes with *such concern* in his own. And it made me cry all the more, realizing how many times he must have hurried to his previous 'mommy' if he heard her crying. Apparently Schatzi does this sort of 'work' in other dimensions too, as I heard;

Schatzi specializes. He has had certain experiences and works with dogs and cats that are experiencing ~ similar traumas, is not too strong a word. There is a certain frequency their grief or anxiety emits into the ethers which resonates instantly with Schatzi, and he is there beside them. This is possible when you understand that time and space are a humanly created convenience, a necessity for living in the third dimension. Other scenarios are the same, whether it is a child afloat on the ocean or cattle starving in Africa, there is a specific frequency attached to each dilemma, and those who are programmed to resonate with that cry will answer the call.

Having been an only dog for so much of his life, Schatzi loved interacting with other dogs, and much enjoyed helping me 'pet-sit' a neighbor's three beautiful Shetland Sheepdogs. The first night I kept the little daxies in our bedroom, but the next night all five dogs were loose together. Primrose climbed into the huge square dog bed and examined every nook and cranny. Then she checked out the couch and the rest of the room. I think she was puzzled why she couldn't find any toys and treats! By the time Schatzi checked out the huge square dog bed, the Shelties realized Something was Going On. They all crowded around and looked down at him in their bed in total astonishment! Supremely nonchalant, Schatzi eventually clambered out and disappeared under their legs. The Shelties continued to be *amazed* at the questing dachshunds. 'What *are* you doing?!" they said, "there's nothing to see here. We know. We live here."

Schatzi also participated in and gave memorable advice in some of our animal communication playdays. Participant Michelle held a responsible managerial position and was having difficulty handling her day and organizing all her staff. She asked him for help. What would Schatzi know about such things, I wondered?! Schatzi told her to take her tea-breaks! Apparently, she always worked straight through them. Michelle took his advice, and it worked wonders. A couple of years later I met her in the grocery store, and she mentioned that she sometimes worked at home now, and one day when she was getting stressed and tense, Schatzi's face appeared on her computer screen and said loudly (in her head), *take your tea break!* For months I wondered, how did he do that?! And then I happened to meet Michelle again, and she mentioned that she still had a photo of my garden as her screensaver, and I understood how that might make it easier for Schatzi to project his image into her life.

The dogs tended to encourage us to ask meaningful questions in these classes, and one time when I asked Schatzi why he was itching he said ~ *oh move on!* So I asked him about his future and he said ~ *stay in the present moment!* So I said OK, I'll talk with Galen (Laurie's little dog), and Schatzi said ~ *of course, you talk with your guests!*

One New Year's Day, the two little dachshunds were curled up together in the big leather recliner for their after-breakfast nap. I sat in front of them, asking and telling them ~ this year I wanted to know and hear more of what they have to say. I was very aware of their bright and shining eyes gazing at me. I felt their thoughts. *Why?* This from Schatzi. *The eyes. We speak through the eyes.* And then, more as if he was talking to himself, *they speak Love. The language of Love.* And even more softly and far away, *and that is all there is.*

> "An animal's eyes have the power to speak a great language."
> ~ Martin Buber

And on Thanksgiving Day, just as Schatzi was making himself comfortable in one of his little cuddler beds, I became acutely aware of his purpose, his service, his reason for being, and heard;

They come as conduits. Conduits for Divine Love, Peace, Joy, Fun ~ whatever the Quality of the Angelic Ray or Realm they represent or from which they emanate. Perhaps they come to bring this quality to the family with which they reside, perhaps to an individual. Schatzi came in Service to Divine Love. His agreement, to give and receive, to be a transmitter, a transducer of this Love to those in need. And because they do come in sentient form, they, these animals, may and will develop their own personalities and feeling tones, adding their own vibratory colors you might say. Very simple in presentation, extremely intricate in concept.

"I so loved being with Shatzi. I felt an emotional and physical shift as he melted into my heart," said our friend Debbie, who had been sitting on the couch holding Schatzi to her chest. And I heard him say, *I am here only to be truly helpful. Anything that I can do to help another, let me do it here and now, for I shall not pass this way again.*

> "The animal has learned to feel,
> but man has come to earth to think.
> Man learns, while angels Serve.
> Serving is higher than ordinary learning.
> The disciple studies, but the Master serves."
> ~ *Peter Deunov (Beinsa Douno) 1864 – 1945*

In accordance with this concept, Schatzi took it upon himself to let me know whenever Primrose (or he), needed something. It probably started when they were outside, and I was a bit slow to let them back in the house. He barks loudly if Primrose is out there by herself. He knows when she has come to the door and is waiting for it to magically open. She will not bark herself and I have to make frequent and constant checks between the back and front door to see where she is, so it is a great help that Schatzi would know and sound the alert ~ which evolved into a dreadful high-pitched staccato sound we called the Schatzi Shriek.

My notes read; this year Primrose is squirrel crazy. With all the doors shut, she knows they are *out there!* And she wants out and at 'em. And if I am not standing at the ready when she has finished her chase, there is the Schatzi Shriek ~ *Primrose needs in!* And I 'hear' him thinking, *Nice day! She tells me I am a Good Boy. And the Princess seems to appreciate me too. I think they really need me; they don't seem able to open doors and things without me giving them clues. I had a nice little chew on the Princess's Bones last night. Very nice of her to let me do this.*

Like all the little dachshunds before him, Schatzi was obsessed with the vegetable garden, his specialty being the little cherry tomatoes. He loved the little cherry tomatoes, especially picking them for himself. One day when we were all outside doing garden things, I heard the Schatzi Shriek. Multiple Schatzi Shrieks! He had eaten all the low growing red ones and was trapped and tangled by clusters of little green ones. By the time I found my camera, he had figured out how to stand on his hind legs, paws resting on the wire cage, and help himself to the next ripened layer!

On another occasion, Primrose was helping me in the garden, but Schatzi preferred to stay snoozing in his little bed on the deck. HA! As soon as I was out of sight he trotted out to the cherry tomatoes and brought himself back a little stash to enjoy in comfort. Another time, when I was up a ladder, Schatzi meandered past with a *huge* red tomato in his mouth ~ *oh no! Where is he going?!* OH YES! Into the house of course, to eat his afternoon snack in the comfort and safety of his little bed under the computer table.

~ ~ ~ ~ ~

Schatzi enjoyed his life to the very end. He came full circle to being an only dog again and we became ever more loving and attentive to each other's needs. He was slowing down, but still loved pottering around in the garden, visiting the neighbors and going in and out of Laurie's doggie door. We focused on appreciating every day he was with us.

And then one afternoon when we had just come in from the garden, I was at the computer, and Schatzi had settled onto one of his little blankets ~ he arose and came to show me his breathing had quickened, and his tummy was expanding. As I phoned the vet to say an emergency was on the way, I was thinking of how I would pick him up. He would be more comfortable if I carried him in one of the little cuddler beds rather than being tucked under my arm ~ and was stunned to see that he had already gone to his little bed while I was on the phone. This would not have been unusual except that he had not been getting in it much lately. It was as if he remembered seeing me carry Primrose to the vet and back in this little bed, and now he knew it was his turn. The vet said he was already in heart failure and gently helped him on his way.

Once again, I phoned good friend and neighbor Neil who had assisted with all the other little dachshunds and two hours later, six of his friends gathered for *The Earthing of Schatzi* ~ with lots of flowers and five of his oh so favorite organic cherry tomatoes. And all the horses stood as sentinels on the hilltop, silhouetted against the glorious sunset in honor of their little friend. I continued to gaze at the glowing kaleidoscope of rainbow colors ~ where is he? Where did Schatzi go? And I sensed a vast unit of energy, a Forcefield of Goodness, and this Forcefield could project parts of itself here, there, or wherever it was needed, in whatever form was most appropriate. Schatzi had simply flowed into, returned to, and become part of this Great Presence of Golden Goodness.

I wrote to his family and friends who could not be present for his Earthing Ceremony;

Schatzi's beautiful brave heart has finally stopped beating and I really miss him. Six weeks after Primrose left us. Of course I always tried to give them equal time, but Schatzi became very, very special and I really understood how much he meant to Helga. He was everywhere with me in the garden, and mostly in the recliner chair with me instead of his own little beds in the house. Because of his heart, we have been expecting him to go for the last two years when he nearly died after a dental, but in two or three months he was fine again. He had a checkup in February and the vet said no more anesthetics, ever. In fact, his previous vet was heard to say that she prayed every night she would never have to do this dog's teeth again! Gallant gentleman that he was, we believe Schatzi wanted to make sure that Primrose would not be left alone, whereas he knew how to be an 'only dog'. He was twelve years and two months old and expected to die eight years ago. Remembrance of Schatzi's life continues to touch the hearts of so many.

"I want you to know that I said goodbye to Shatzi the other day. I told him that he had done a wonderful job here on earth, that he was very brave, and that everything would be ok. He loved Helga and knew she loved him, but he did wonder, what did he do wrong that she left him? It helped him so much to be here. It was his time." ~ *Melissa*

"Oh, how very beautiful. I'm so deeply moved. What a great service. I can feel his comforting love across the ethers. Thank you for reminding me about the wonderful story of Schatzi's life. I met him years ago when we visited your lovely home." ~ *Nancy*

"It was wonderful being a part of Schatzi's Earthing Ceremony with the setting sun. Thank you for letting me participate." ~ *Mary Lee*

"What an inspiration his life has been." ~ *Michele*

"Now who is going to watch out for the aliens in my yard?!" ~ *Laurie*

"It meant so much, sharing in Schatzi's Earthing Ceremony." ~ Candace-Two-Legs

"I don't think I've ever heard quite such a lovely story. Do you think God will give Schatzi a doggie door? I think so, and cherry tomatoes too. I'll always think of him when I eat one." ~ Pat

I continue to remind people that Schatzi is *Love in Service*, and that they can call upon him to escort their own animals (and humans) 'over the Rainbow Bridge'. As an example, I share the following story.

Several of us were volunteering at the local animal shelter and to our great distress, our five favorite dogs were to be euthanized. Mattie was a beautiful little black and tan five-year-old coonhound whom I used to visit and take for walkies every day. I told Schatzi what was about to happen, and asked if he would escort Mattie to the Other Side. At the appointed hour I was driving my car and thinking about Mattie and had a sudden vision of her standing in front of me, with a great vibrational river flowing swift and strong and beautiful in front of her. On the other side, lined up along the bank, were hundreds of dogs of all shapes and colors and sizes, all wagging their tails and laughing happily. At their center, stood a great and wondrous light filled cream colored Golden Retriever. Mattie's pack were waiting for her!

Later, I asked Schatzi if he had indeed escorted her to the other side. He said, *I didn't have to take her all the way.* I assumed that meant he too had seen her Pack and knew that she would be alright. When I got home, there was a message on the answering machine saying the event had been delayed until the next day.

"I am communicating with Schatzi and have asked him to be an escort for my cat Pumpkin as she makes her transition." ~ Judy

And then one day, I heard within my mind, that Schatzi was not just 'an escort', he was one of *The Escorts*. Schatzi himself speaks, as one of The Escorts;

We created a Forcefield of energy in Spirit, you could call it an Angel, for it will be embodied. But first we must create it, and the more who offer their energy and support, the stronger and greater it will grow. A blessing some might term it, from those who were in canine form to protect, to help, and assist in whatever manner ~ Life in distress or limitation. And here, we are working with those who have chosen to serve Humanity as guards and guides, officers and medics, to help the weak and ailing. We can be called upon, not only to offer our support to those, our companions in form, but to welcome them home. This happens anyway of course, but we will be as a specialized unit.

Schatzi and his Unit of Love in Service are also in Service to the Service Dogs. He and his Team may be called upon to escort both humans and animals to the worlds beyond. Events like 9/11 and other catastrophes came to mind.

Shatzi has retained consciousness of his own essence,
and although he may not use his actual Schatzi template again,
his own particular essence could be recognized as such,
for he is one in Service to Love, ever ready to flow as needed.

The following quote refers to "the Star of Spiritual Freedom that may be presented as a Star Forcefield in any configuration or geometry that the seer 'sees'." For me, it explains how Schatzi's *Love in Service Forcefield* may express parts, or units of itself in any way or manner appropriate for the occasion.

The nature of Spiritual Freedom is not locked into a pre-set pattern,
but rather serves the moment, with as many points to the Star as desired,
or required for perfect Light Service in any moment.
It is an ever-changing, Eternal Moment of Light Service.
~ Ascended and Free

Schatzi was the last of the ten little dachshunds.

The Flame 1995

The first I knew about The Flame was when a friend suddenly asked, "What's this about a flame that Gretel and Heidi have handed to Tiggy, and that Loreli desires so much to be worthy of receiving?" As soon as Janet left, I asked to be given insights as to the nature and function of this Flame. I am told it is a Flame that Gretel brought to life.

It is a Flame that Gretel exuded from her own heartlight to blaze on everlasting, to bear the essence, the frequency of her Homeland, for it is more, this Flame, than the essence of her own High Self, it is the quintessence of that place from whence she came. And Gretel so loved the world that she would gift it to this land, to the beings of this land in which she knew so much joy, so much happiness, so much caring and love.

It is her gift, and Heidi (her daughter) has expanded, has added to this Flame and it has grown. And because it contains their heart gifts, the heart gifts of both ~ is why they both work with Tiggy in enabling her to support and carry this mighty Flame, for it does grow, and other ones (Beings of Light) are adding to its force, are feeding it their own Light. And it has become a great and mighty power. And it must have one in form to hold it in this realm. Thus do they both work with Tiggy, for she could not hold it by herself.

And Loreli indeed, shall be a very worthy and magnificent bearer of this torch. In fact she may even now assist Tiggy in holding it on line. It is anchored through Tiggy's heart into this Earth, into this place (the Garden of Sananda), and it penetrates deep into the Earth Star's heart. Thus is it available to each and every realm through which it passes in the inner realms, the inner earth. It is like a source of nutrients to those who would partake.

Its color would appear to be crystalline, opalescent perhaps, for when you watch you see the colors of the rainbows that you view within your crystals, dancing in the shimmering Flame. For the Flame is a concentration of vibration in the form of flame. And this Flame does not move with Tiggy wherever she goes, no ~ it is anchored through the garden, and she is more, if you would be technical, the Guardian, the Caretaker, the appointed Keeper of this Flame. But it was handed to her, thus is she referenced as the Bearer or Carrier of the Torch. ~ God bless.

And I was given the understanding that Tiggy was now the apex of this Flame, this *Pyramid of Light* that has been building in size and power ever since its creation, and that Heidi, who had been holding this position was now able to go further and higher and deeper into the Great Silence, because Tiggy had taken her place. The word 'filter' came to mind, *Tiggy is a filter* through which Heidi can blaze ever stronger emanations of her Power and Glory. She can now fine focus her attention through Tiggy, rather than hold the entire Pyramidal Flame herself. Subconsciously, I already knew this, but now it seemed like a sealing of this image. Later I realized this was also referencing the portal opening through the Heart of Sananda, from the Celestial Realms to the Earth Star's Heart. Portals within portals.

> "Absolutely beautiful.
> Your vortex is blessing the earth.
> May other vortices arise,
> kindled by Sananda's Flame and join,
> together ~ as One."
> ~ *blessings, blessings, blessings, Crystal*

Soon after this we had an Animal Communication Playday. We included a meditation and invitation to all and any animals who needed help in moving on, who might be stuck in or around the earth realm. On this occasion, everyone saw Gretel's Flame, the vibrational pyramidal *Flame of Love,* and we felt many, many animals from the disasters of Kosovo, and humans too, were released through this Point of Power. And someone saw Tiggy sitting in the middle of the Pyramid, sweetly content on her little green beanie bag!

~ ~ ~ ~ ~

The years passed. And Tiggy celebrated her 17th Birthday Party. She really didn't celebrate much, but she did have a party and a carrot cake and lots of edible presents, most of which she will donate to the local animal shelter. Tiggy is doing well but she sleeps a great deal. Many feel her tiredness. Many refer to her as the Wise One. Lorna likes to sleep with her, curled around her. A few weeks ago, animal communicator

Donna Marie was visiting and picked up something about a flame being passed (again). She knew nothing of the above story. Immediately I felt that it was being passed to Lorna and Loreli, and that Candace would very soon become a third corner, for now I was sensing it as a tetrahedron, a three sided pyramid. Tiggy would then be the capstone in spirit. I asked for more information. I ask of Infinite Intelligence;

You ask why Tiggy sleeps so much. 90% of the time, although she is not unwell. She is transferring the energies of this Flame she has held so long. She is tired. Not of her duties, but of the involvement and attention required from such a high-powered project. Gretel birthed it, this Flame. It was her gift ~ conceived in joy, presented with Love. For her it was a creation she could enjoy and savor, for it was a celebration of her life on Earth. Heidi was present at the creation; Heidi grew with the Flame and inherited it as a daughter inherits her mother's wealth. And as Heidi grew in strength and stature, so did the Flame. Gently and with great Love did she (Heidi) train the new young fledgling that you called Tiggy. And by the time Heidi departed, Tiggy was fully able to step into her position as Keeper of the Flame. Guardian of the Light.

By the time Loreli arrived this Flame was an awesome and wondrous sight for one so small. And she had doubts as to her own ability to inherit and sustain such might. Thus Lorna was drawn to the circle, the spiral. You were surprised she came, and now there were three. And Lorna was as an anchor, a support to ground these ever increasing and powerful energies. And as the time draws nigh for Beloved Tiggy to take her place by Heidi's side in Spirit, so was Candace drawn to the front lines. For what Candace lacks in current awareness, she makes up for in youth and vigor and astuteness and will hold her point of this Pyramid of Light we call The Flame, with courage and fortitude.

I had sent friend Jim an old photo of Tiggy and Heidi sitting together in front of the statue of Saint Francis. Jim had a very special rapport with Loreli, he knew Tiggy well, and had been the only other person to see Heidi's footsteps in the snow 'that just stopped.' He knew nothing of The Flame but spontaneously replied, *Keepers of The Flame, Guardians of the Light!*

Candace was only five years old when she arrived. I thought about all this. Did other animals create similar Flames? Perhaps if they were given the idea they would do so. Perhaps we could consciously start using this Flame whenever or wherever there is a need, alerting those in difficulties, directing those about to make their transition into its radiance ~ not just wait to do so in our infrequent meditation groups. Perhaps we humans might consider birthing Flames of our own, through our own hearts, from our own Source ~ for purposes that might help the Earth and all Life. And then we must remember to feed these Flames, and perhaps ask others to assist in building and holding and strengthening them. I ask for any comments.

Indeed, this Flame can be used to direct those animals ~ all Life who know or experience trauma, in life or transition, to seek and enter its radiance and move onward in peace. Sananda allowed Gretel a space in which to create this emblem of her Love. Remember, this was a Flame of Love birthed in loving conditions. Mary birthed the Child of Wonder into a barn of animals who knew only peace and acceptance. She did not birth him into the chaos of war and demolition. Such frequencies are supportive to the purity of intent involved in this endeavor. ~ God bless, we are the Brotherhood of Infinite Intelligence.

~ ~ ~ ~ ~

The years flowed on. Ingrid came to visit, ostensibly to do her laundry! Suddenly she started 'channeling' Babaji, and many other Great Beings. The Flame! Yes! It had merged with Sananda, but Ingrid saw it displayed as a Lotus, and each petal as a landing pad for various nature kingdoms, and the center was reserved for the Cetaceans. As each little dachshund came from different frequencies, they had very effectively represented the different directions and locations of their origins, their homelands. Deities manifested as dachshunds!

Next summer, I sat in the hammock with Candace at my feet, thinking of Gretel and Heidi and Tiggy and Loreli and Lorna and Lilly. I got a 'nothing' on Gretel. She has returned to Light and just Is. And yet, she it was who created The Flame. She it was who opened me to my Greater Self. And Heidi ~ I feel Sananda itself *is held within the Heart of Heidi.* Tiggy ~ and I realize, I 'see', that every time a dog leaves, The Flame grows in size and power as it passes from dachshund to dachshund, and as each precious one returns to Spirit, their essence goes into this Flame, this Heartlight ~ in sacred geometries and swirling lights, as a *kaleidoscope of infinite color* creating a moving, dancing matrix that surrounds or holds Sananda in form.

Matrix or matrice, is there a difference? Which do I mean? I look it up in the dictionary: *An enclosure within which something originates or develops. From the Latin for womb.*

> *Sananda has developed within the matrix*
> *formed by Great Ones of Light*
> *who sent their essence to be in form,*
> *for they must be represented in physical form,*
> *as an anchor, a point of focus for the Work involved.*

And now Candace, as the only little dachshund currently in form, is the focus for the earthly tip of this energy, everything depends on her. No wonder we feel so protective of each other. No wonder I feel that she feels such a great responsibility. She has been trained, or brought to her full power, *their* full power, by The Group. They have been creating a bridge, a connecting link. Gretel created The Flame, she laid the foundation, Heidi opened the portal and holds Sananda in her Heartlight, Tiggy brought in the elementals, the fairy kingdoms, Loreli was the ET connection, Lorna was the Open Heart, and sweet Lilly (*I am all brand new, the Lightworkers created me*) lit the fuse and triggered the next step ~ and so much, much more was each. What *is* the next step? Does Candace know?

A message came from Ingrid (after Candace had returned to Spirit); *Your girls, Lorna and Candace, say ~ their spirit is with you today and every day. The Light of this Flame has increased with each one who came, and with each generation has grown stronger and stronger, and will anchor ever more deeply with the little ones to come. They will touch the heart of all and anchor the seeds of receptivity within each person they come in contact with, even those who do not believe that anything of spiritual consequence could be manifested by such little dogs!*

Regarding 'the little ones to come'! The following Spring, after a dachshundless winter, Primrose (who was very little) and her daughter Olivia arrived, and a month or so after that Lorna's grandson Schatzi joined us. Presumably Gretel's Flame was now self-sustaining, self-existing and on automatic, and Primrose had other duties to attend! I was informed that she had come to 'gather up all the messages'! The DNA imprints left across the land by all the other little dachshunds. This kept her very busy!

Meanwhile, Ingrid keeps *nearly* letting go of her ancient Siamese cat Pookah and asked me to tune in to his thoughts and feelings. I was promptly reminded of The Flame, and asked Pookah if he knew of or had perhaps created such a thing himself. He said, *of course, all of us did* (meaning the other animals in his house, dog and more cats). And I had a vision of Bella the Great Dane, big and sparkling black and white. So luminously clear and vibrant. She and Candace had a close bond, seemingly a soul connection. Ingrid said Candace had given Bella back her wings the first time they met. Had Candace told her about The Flame?

~ ~ ~ ~ ~

Decades later, I was still receiving snippets of insights and understandings that The Flame continues to evolve. Opening, expanding, causing renewal, creating patterns of perfection, working in conjunction with the DNA created by the movements of Paneurhythmy, the joyous and sacred meditational dance from the Celestial realms that we do barefoot in the garden ~ anchoring and broadcasting the spiritual meaning and qualities within the movements to the worlds around, and deep into the Earth herself.

2023 ~ Thirty Years Later

On Easter Sunday, as I was doing my morning meditation
and declaring the portals of Sananda open,
ready, and available ~ to give and to receive
the greatest Light possible,
I became aware of the entire Garden of Sananda,
the entire Sanctuary or Space of Love,
encompassed in a great blazing Golden Light
that I knew as
Gretel's Ascension Flame.

The Ascension of Others

They come to earth as raindrops do.
Touch lightly in this realm
and bless all ones who knew
the Wonder of their Love.

The Ascension of Emma 2019

Emma was a petite and adorable little Norwich Terrier who lived with me as my own little dog when her human was away working and travelling. Emma was a magnet for children to pet and a comfort for the elderly to hold. Earlier I heard, that like Beloved Schatzi, Emma was Love in Service. She supported her human through many moves and changes.

Emma is Love in Service and represents continuity.
She will stay as long as her Presence is needed.
Not by you, but by the one she came to Serve.
To Serve in Love.
For you, she is a gift.

At 18 years old Emma attained her Freedom. Eventually I asked her if she would give me words or thoughts on how things are with her now;

You may think of me as Light for I am formless. I flow with the heart songs. As the need comes, there I am, and yes, I can be everywhere. I am with you when you think of me, my presence indicating comfort which may manifest as happy memories, or movements that make you smile, lighten and brighten the hour. And the same of course, for my Beloved, the one who gave me space to Be. Whenever there is a need wherever my presence can bring ease, there I AM. Think not of me as a little dog, but rather as a frequency, a specific frequency that you interpret as Emma. For That I AM. God bless.

The Ascension of Digit 1995

Digit was an adventurous little kitten whose life ended abruptly. He knew no fear ~ he had no sense! He lost track of his nine lives and attempted one adventure too many.

>Will o'the wisp, a Child of Light am I.
>Dancing through Life ~ in form or out,
>it matters not to me.
>Free as the ocean waves, the clouds themselves am I.
>Tasting, sensing, feeling ~ I tred the different paths in joy.
>Ever in rhythm, ever by choice ~ I AM eternal.
>a song within a dream.
>Come sing my song and dance with me
>for yesterday is here no more,
>and tomorrow lies formless in the void,
>but today I AM and call to you
>to sing my song across the waves,
>an echo from the toning stars.
>Digit flies free ~ a sound within the Silence
>that came to Earth as raindrops do.
>A blessing to be known within the moment
>and released in Love.

The Ascension of Tiny Mike 1987

Tiny Mike was a very small and very elderly black and white pony who had been with my neighbor since she was a baby. He lived with various other horses and when he lost most of his teeth, she made him a special easy-to-eat messy mash, which of course the other horses wanted too. So a bar was placed across the barn door which was easy for Tiny Mike to walk under, and his friends just had to stand and watch him eat ~ slowly!

One happy Easter Sunday morning, he was loaded into the trailer and taken down the road to a little country church for a Blessing of the

Animals. He was a star! A great favorite among the dogs and cats and a hermit crab. Early one winter's morn I found him lying close beside my garden fence, his little nose pointing to the East.

No more an elderly pet pony,
beloved though he may have been.
Your Tiny Mike flies free on rainbow trails,
through golden acres of fresh flowers,
and not alone.
For the Great Herd of the East he knows as his
have come to welcome him.

On wings of Light they come.
Through sun kissed clouds to greet the Dawn
and bring him Home.
For Horses of the East are leaders
in bringing the Light, the Dawn,
the awakening of New Thought
within the mind of man.

With honors has Tiny Mike fulfilled his task.
And now ~ a spirit horse of crystal light,
with silver wings he flows
through waves of grace,
and dances through the mists of time.
His heart re-tuned and beating
to the rhythm of the stars,
reverberating to the song Creation sings.
Your Tiny Mike is, was and ever shall be loved,
a star amongst the stars.
A heartbeat in the Heart of God.

The Ascension of Amanda 1995

I received a request for information on what happened to Amanda, a cat who had been found fifteen years earlier as a small straggly grey kitten crawling around the garbage bins in a garage. Now, she had disappeared ~ just disappeared, from her back doorstep. I ask for insight on what truly happened, words that would help her person understand and bring peace, words that would expand her consciousness and give higher meaning to what had occurred.

And I am given the image of a black, black sky with pinpoints of brilliant stars. And silhouetted before me is the outline of a cat sitting upright, ears perked. Staring into the void, into the blackness, into the far beyond;

And Amanda knows, Amanda knows that she is to return from whence she came, that it is time for her to leave. And so she waits, knowing her friends will come and take her home as they promised they would do before she entered form. Thus did they place her down and thus will they take her home. In a whirling vortex of energy was Amanda drawn into their midst. And it was not for her to worry about how she would be missed. It was not for her to be concerned about what would occur after she had left. For Amanda had fulfilled her mission and it was time for her to return to Spirit. To the great fiery Light she knew before she commenced her dream spell upon Star Terra, Planet Earth. And Amanda's welcome home was joyous. Amanda was greeted as a long-lost family member who has been on a secret, sacred, and dangerous mission. For ones of such great Light as she, there are dangers in condensing one's energy and holding a lesser focus for this time period of Service.

And Amanda is still integrating her thoughts, you might term it, back into the Oneness that she knew, that she is. For she is part of a cluster of Star Lights, who serve in form on rare and special occasions. And it is only to rare and special people that they may come. To those who would understand and care for them in a manner and way that would allow them to perform what it is they came to do. And Amanda was an anchor for this Star Light. Amanda served as a living vortex to anchor the energies of her Star Light cluster, into the Earth.

And so you might say she came to heal, she was a healer. And the one to whom she came is a part of this Service also of course, and because the connection has been made, this Star Light cluster may continue to blaze their essence through her form and continue the work that Amanda has set in motion. And Amanda would say ~ look not for me upon the Earth, but raise your vision, raise your sight and seek me in the higher realms, for there I AM.

I mailed this off and included the name of another animal communicator. Amanda's person sent a card of a most beautiful red rose and wrote; "Having confirmation of your information from another helped a lot. Amanda had not incarnated before and does not intend to again. She was very concerned that she would not be able to hold the connection when trying to anchor the energies she was bringing in. If she had not been able to hold the connection, she would not have been able to do the work she came to do. And the reason I won't find her body is because she did an 'internal combustion' kind of thing, where she disappeared in a 'flash'. Thank you again for such incredibly beautiful information."

The Ascension of Natty 1984

The following story from a close friend about their little dog Natty is remarkably like *The Ascension of Heidi* ~ the excitement, the insistence to go out, the snow, and the pawprints that just stopped.

"This is the story of our dear Natasha and her transition over the rainbow bridge. She was a little white wire-haired terrier that we adopted after she had a litter of puppies. We took her home the day we went to see her and she became a loving family member in no time at all. She never roamed far from the house and did not like to be left in the yard very long. Natty was thirteen years old, with no sign of any health issues. Winter was coming, temperatures were dropping and there was a dusting of snow around the house, on the front porch and beyond.

We heard strange noises coming from downstairs and went to see what all the commotion was about. Natty was acting in an unusual manner, restless, excited, and running around in circles. It seemed that she wanted out, so we took her upstairs and she quickly went out of the front door. We checked on her very soon, expecting her to be at the door ready to come in. No Natty. Alarmed, we hurried to check the back door. No Natty. We continued calling and checking all the doors. Ten minutes passed, still no Natty. The dusting of snow was still visible and now we noticed Natty's paw prints going to the end of the porch, down the steps, into the parking area and a short distance down a slight incline of the drive. We couldn't figure out why her tracks 'stopped'. They didn't go any farther. No tracks coming back. What happened? We searched the entire property and beyond. Natty never went far from the house, and the driveway was over 100 feet long. No one would come up the drive to take her, and anyway the snow was undisturbed from where her tracks stopped.

Even now, we still find Natty's disappearance a mystery. *She was so anxious to go outside.* We have heard of other pets just vanishing with no trace. Going over the rainbow bridge instantaneously seems to be what can happen. This may have happened to Natty. Taken into the heavenly realms body and soul in an instant." ~ *Lorraine*

Part Two
Ascension Related Concepts

The word 'Ascension' undoubtedly means different things to different people. Following is a collection of quotes, notes and comments related to the meaning of Ascension as portrayed in The Ascension of Heidi.

"Ascension is the highest possible outcome for every person, place, condition and thing, at any given moment." ~ *Ascended and Free*

Ascension is transformation, transition.
A change in way of being. A change in consciousness
to a higher harmonic frequency that causes molecular transformation.
Ascension is a joyful culmination of a life well lived.
And like most things ~ Ascension is a multifaceted Truth,
With many interpretations and ways of presentation.

"In the past Ascension was understood as a physical departure or lift off from earth. The third-dimensional view. Now, a Fifth-Dimensional view reveals it rather as a Supreme Light emanating from within and from within all form and matter around you. It assimilates all life on Earth into its own perfection within, without that life going anywhere. The Ascension is taking place continuously within all life. The Earth simply emerges into the highest perfection of Herself, enfolded in and embraced by the Light radiating from the atoms that compose Her as well as the Sun that shine upon Her surface." ~ *Group Avatar*

"Ascension is a method of consciously moving from one world to another, taking your body with you." ~ *Nothing in This Book Is True, But It's Exactly How Things Are by Bob Frissell*

According to Hindu philosophy, if the body should become nearly 100% sattva, embodying the virtues of light, goodness and purity, it will vanish into light ~ Ascension. In Sanskrit this is termed Dehamukti.

"The complete metamorphosis of matter into light
is a very advanced form of ascension,
and is generally only seen in highly developed Initiates."
~ A Hathor Planetary Message through Tom Kenyon

"Ascension is the mastery of self, time and space.
Living free of self, time and space,
yet choosing the freedom to live within self, time and space,
in Service to the Earth and Humanity." ~ Ascended and Free

"Ascension is multi-dimensional identity integration." ~ Phil Gruber

"Standing in the Light,
one may choose to disappear into Infinite Flowing Wholeness,
or one may choose to reappear
in perfect form and function within daily life."
~ Ascended and Free

For some, Ascension means learning to vibrate at a higher frequency so that we can live in a different dimension on this planet, without leaving this Earth realm. Accomplished, or at least quickened, by living a life of gratitude, kindness, compassion, and consideration for others ~ for all Life. Being consciously aware at all times, of spiritual thoughts and deeds that may accelerate soul growth.

Ascension may be seen as an ongoing evolutionary process of body, mind and spirit into one's highest potential. A process in which the physical body eventually becomes fused or united with its counterpart of Light. A process that refers to all physical matter, including the Earth herself, and is inevitable whether one believes it or not. A process that may be quickened or accelerated by our own intent, and living in a manner that supports health, wellness and conscious Light Being. ~ from the Sananda Ascension Essence manual, replicated in Whale Wisdom Dolphin Joy

Ascension is matter transmuting into energy, collapsing in upon itself and dissolving. Vibrating the subatomic particles so fast that they evolve into energy.

Ascension ~ a process of raising the frequencies of the physical body to merge with the lightbody. 'En-lightening' the body so that we can radiate the divine light through each of our cells, transforming the physical body into a body of light.

Jivanmukti; Jiva, meaning 'life,' and mukti, meaning 'freedom', in the Vedanta philosophy indicates the attainment of self-realization, spiritual liberation, enabling limitless knowledge and eternal bliss while still consciously living in form ~ Ascension.

The side effects of Ascension may vary according to the nature of the one ascending. It could be unmitigated joy; it could be withdrawal into a deeper peace than has ever been experienced; it could express as spontaneous and unexpected love and appreciation for all ~ Reverence for Life. Or it might be quiet acknowledgement, the recognition of beauty and innocence within the core of all things. Ascension empowers the ability to encompass all experiences with compassion and understanding, a silent call for all to surrender to the path of Peace, Love and Light. ~ God bless, we are the Brotherhood, the Brotherhood of Angels and of Men (Humanity).

Regarding the fact that I forever thought of Heidi as 'pure Spirit', an angel and my equal, the following quote seemed to help clarify my understanding of this:

"Spirit (Eternal Flame as Divine Consciousness and Cohesive Vibration) chooses to become manifest as Divinely Intelligent Matter, it's expression of Light." ~ *Ascended and Free*

"Ascension brings each carbon atom through spiritual metamorphosis, dramatically accelerating its Vibration into the essence of a Diamond. Then, each photon that makes up the Ascended Presence gives off the Cosmic Radiance of Infinity, each 'Diamond' filled with the limitless Light potential of the universal I AM ~ on Earth! This parallel universe is the Infinite Circle of Light, bearing the name of the Silent Watcher of the Universe, Lady Circulata. Ascension from completely carbon based to completely Light based will occur gradually, without outer cataclysmic activity." ~ *Ascended and Free*

NOTE: I, Sananjaleen, saw myself thus after taking Power and Glory, a vibrational essence I was guided to make in the Garden of Sananda.

Suddenly, without warning or expectation, I momentarily experienced myself as composed of a myriad brilliant tiny crystalline diamond lights.

Also, after she returned to Spirit, I occasionally saw Gretel thus, in my meditations. I would think of her as being in her Radiant or Diamond Body. At other times she was like crystal glass, which at that time, I called her 'see-through' body, and much later realized was probably her 5th-Dimensional Crystalline Solar Light Body.

"The process of Redemption, Transformation and Ascension occur when the 'particle-function' (underlying the manifestation of matter and substance) begins to accelerate in Energy, Vibration and Consciousness towards its Original 'wave-function ~ Perfection Patterns'!" ~ *Ascended and Free*

"One of the primary components of Christ Consciousness (Ascension) is harmonization, which involves unification of the physical and subtle bodies, anchoring the spiritual realm into the physical realm, right down to the cellular level." ~ *Virginia Essene*

"Ascension is our next evolutionary step, and everyone on Earth must eventually make the Ascension. It requires a deep inner understanding, acknowledgement, love and constant communion with our own individualized I AM Presence, as through this Mighty I AM Presence we can call forth the Light Rays to redeem and set free all misuse of life back to the beginning of time, balance our use of life over many lifetimes, and purify our four Earthly bodies and thus qualify for the Ascension." ~ *Anthea Torr*

"The opportunity to ascend from within the 'density of form' is unique in all the Solar System, and since the 'great fall' in consciousness, an even more 'extraordinary endeavor than ever designed for." ~ *Ascended and Free*

"We are here to Master 'particle-function form and make our Ascension back to 'wave-function' Spirit, back to our Electronic Mighty I AM Presence in the Realms of Light. It (the Eternal Flame) proceeds through these Cosmic Cycles and may express as 'wave-function' or 'particle-function' or not express individually at all, and simply exist in the Great Solar Quiet within the endless Ocean of Nirvana." ~ *Ascended and Free*

"For a mass to travel faster than light, it would simply have to achieve wholeness with the universal structure, which is not a question of speed, but of identification with form. It is a matter of becoming one with the light. Identification with light is the key to transcending form and speed." ~ *Saryon Michael White*

"If the choice was to ascend our physical bodies, we could increase the frequency of the physical elements in such a way that we disappeared from the earth plane, thus ascending the physical elements of the Earth to the 'other side of the veil'. And although my outer eyes did not see her glorious Ascension, my inner eyes beheld an expanding globe of brilliant white light move out from her heart center. I felt the very molecules of her body quicken and restructure into a much more refined form as she merged with a spiraling light. Then, as if the wind suddenly exploded with a whoosh through a vacuum, she was lifted up." She was also guided to go to a special place. ~ *from Anna the Grandmother of Jesus in regard to her daughter's Ascension.*

Regarding the option of ascending the physical body or not; "If we chose to consciously slip our light body out of the physical focus, the physical elements that were 'left behind' were charged with higher states of ascend consciousness. Our interred bodies would continue to radiate benevolent blessings into the Earth Mother to assist her eventual ascension. If we chose to ascend our physical bodies, we could increase the frequency of the physical elements in such a way that we disappeared from the earth plane, thus ascending the physical elements of the Earth to the 'other side of the veil'". ~ *from Anna the Grandmother of Jesus.*

NOTE: Regarding the phrase 'our interred bodies would continue to radiate benevolent blessings into the Earth Mother', when Loreli died, instead of burying her beneath the Pines with the other little dachshunds, the gnomes notified me that they wanted her in their Gnome Sanctuary which also consisted of Pine trees, but in a different area. I received the impression that this, the receiving of Loreli's body into their sanctuary, was a long-awaited day of joyous celebration. The day after we placed her there, marked by a large Elestial crystal, Lorna and I were sitting in silence when the gnomes gave me an image of many of them coming from far and wide with their little wheelbarrows, gathering precious essence from Loreli's body. And I was reminded of the saying; *The relics of the saints are more precious than silver and gold.*

Build walls of Light and spheres of Love around yourselves, and nothing that does not resonate with your own Heartsong may enter in. This is Ascension ~ ascension from all that binds, restricts or limits the feel, expression and knowing of That I AM ~ whatever term or word you choose to call the Eternal Flame of All Creation.

Regarding 'the Resurrection of the Christ': "If we take the event literally, Jesus as the Christ was able to convert the matter-energy garment of ascension, subsequently disappearing from this reality and leaving no matter or energy behind. In a true sense, matter was transformed into Light, and we would contest that it was not simply photonic light with a small 'l', but Light with a capital 'L', supraliminal Light, which is a greater Light that can manifest and demanifest in our local life space, as well as interpenetrate our conscious thought." ~ *The Gospel of Mary* by Dr J. J. Hurtak and Dr Desiree Hurtak.

Another text from the Gospel mentions: "Usually the manifestation of any 'Whole Light Being' from a higher realm is not only overwhelming for the experience itself, but it is accompanied by an energy frequency that can overwhelm us on this side of physical reality. This applies also to what the Kabbalists call the Merkabah experience. In addition to the appearance is the energy field that is the open link between our world and other realms Light, for it is truly part of the opening of the heavenly dimensions that takes place." ~ *The Gospel of Mary* by Dr J. J. Hurtak and Dr Desiree Hurtak.

NOTE: This describes so well the overwhelm I experienced when Gretel came to me as Light. When she told me, *I too have returned to the Light, I too AM THAT I AM.* And 'witnessing' the awesomeness of little Primrose returning to Love.

In the book *The Law of One, The Ra Material*, there is reference to 'The Harvest' after we have learned or attained the frequency of Love. Perhaps this may also be interpreted as 'The Ascension'. The book also suggests that truth offered without proof can act as a motivator to seek and find, a self-empowerment that automatically increases the vibratory rate of the seeker.

"For as soon as the expanding Eternal Flame 'touches the garment' of the Mantle of Light around our embodied presence at its level of Energy, Vibration and Consciousness, then Transfiguration into the Light Body begins in earnest. This is the sign that the embodied individual has expanded their Light, their Divine Instrument, their True Identity enough so that they have earned to once again be 'anointed' into the Kingdom of Heaven ~ while still embodied!" ~ *Ascended and Free*

The Concept of Ascension in Relation to Gravity

In accordance with the teachings of the Ascended Masters, so beautifully presented in the website www.ascendedandfree.org it is mentioned that Ascension is the process that breaks the bonds of gravity. Ascension releases us from the bonds of the third dimension, allowing us to consciously experience our multi-dimensional realities.

"The Ascension Flame is the antidote to gravity!"
~ *Ascended and Free*

"Ascension reverses the effect of gravity in our physical, etheric, mental and emotional bodies. Ascension is Cause and gravity is effect. Gravity 'marries' us to third dimensional form. Reversing gravity on a physical, etheric, mental and emotional level is now the purpose of Standing in the Light. Just as gravity is an essential foundation of physics of our old dimension, orbit or reality, the Ascension is an essential foundation of physics of the New Dimension, Orbit and Reality of Earth."
~ *Ascended and Free*

"When an individual has governed time and space through being empty of self, then gravity is something to be 'mastered' rather than something that automatically governs us. This is the physical representation of the Ascension, someone literally rising off the planet.

It actually represents an Enlightened Being rising out of self, time and space and into Higher Dimensions, all available in the present, right here and now." ~ *Ascended and Free*

"The Ascension Flame reverses the effect of gravity. Spiritual gravity (or inertia) pulls us back to old ego habits, just as physical gravity pulls us to the ground. The Cohesive Power of Divine Love is a Forcefield that transforms separateness into Wholeness, fulfilling our Unity with Divine Potential. When in Union with God Self, we think Ascended and Free; we feel Ascended and Free; we remember Ascended and Free; and we act Ascended and Free! Ascension is Cause and gravity is effect (of non-ascension).

Thus, the Gathering of Ascended Humanity 'gathers' all life energies within the Cohesive Power of Divine Love, reversing gravity on a physical, etheric, mental and emotional level. This authorizes all life to proceed upwards in vibration, (rather than upward in space), towards its Divine Potential. We then remain 'on Earth' not because of gravity (or spiritual inertia) but because of our Ascended and Free intention and free will to serve life here." ~ *The Flame of Purity, Ascended and Free*

In my small paperback *The Dolphin Ones,* I describe an occasion where they gave me an image of themselves rising out of the ocean to greet the star ships, it took me decades to realize this was a demonstration of their mastery. Mastery over 3D existent. They were showing me, or I was allowed to see, their mastery over time, space, and gravity ~ their ability to rise or ascend off this planet into a Higher Dimension.

"In metaphysical science, Ascension is that Force which governs or 'masters' gravity, a fundamental principle of the Universe. According to Einstein's Theory of General Relativity, gravity is the only force woven through all dimensions of time and space and cannot be confined to any particular universe, whether that universe has three dimensions or twenty. In metaphysical terms, the Ascension is the opposite and balancing force to gravity and once achieved, governs it and everything it influences. So when Beloved Jesus or the Prophet Mohammed 'ascended', there was a physical lifting off the Earth witnessed by others. What we really achieve from the Ascension is the Spiritual Freedom to exist anywhere within or beyond time and space, without necessarily going anywhere. Ascension is a state of Divine Consciousness secured by the greatest unifying Force in the Universe, the Cohesive Power of Divine Love sustaining all life in her Ascended State." ~ *Ascended and Free*

"In scientific terms, in quantum physics, gravitation is one of the four primary forces that govern 'reality' in the physical realm. Once the seven planetary Chakras are mastered, the Root Chakra then grants the final act of the Ascension allowing an Ascended and Free being to govern gravitational force, rather than being governed by it. Gravitational force, when mastered, takes us beyond time and space, into countless other dimensions." ~ *Ascended and Free*

"Lightness ~ a new relationship with gravity." ~ *Michio Kaku*

~ ~ ~ ~ ~

Anticipating questions that people may ask! How can I explain ~ 'what is Ascension'?

You may say that Ascension is a process, a natural process of evolution. As a flower comes to full bloom, so do different lifestreams come to their Ascension, to the point of their Ascension. Meaning that it is time for the next step in the evolution of a given race. In this case, all lifestreams upon the Earth planet, and the planet herself have come to the point of Ascension.

What does that mean? Because the flower itself will die.

It is a process of dying to the old ways and all that they represent.

Including the limitations of the physical form?

This is the excitement created by the idea, the talk, the thought of Ascension ~ the perfection of your physical bodies, because you live in a physical world and are preoccupied with such. But there is far more attached to the process of Ascension than simply the transformation of the physical body into one of unlimited perfection, known as your light body or Merkabah. And the Merkabah is not exactly the same, it is more of a ~ collective, is the word that comes to mind, and yet it is individual also.

And if they ask, what do I have to do, how can I ascend? How shall I answer?

In fact, they do not have to do anything except be willing and allow the changes that flow through their life. And they will have the choice whether to accept them and go with the flow, or whether to battle and fight for the old ways.

And those that fight and battle for the old ways, will they not ascend?

They will of course eventually ascend, but they will not be part of your Wave. They may be seen, the different levels of consciousness and willingness, as waves. And the first wavers will be those that support the system of the Ascension process. And the others will be as in a holding pattern and must wait until the next opportunity ~ which may be a very long time.

Ascension creates upliftment and joy and new hope. It is something to aspire to, and if the next rung is too far, or the next step too high, look around and ask, ask how you may proceed. There will be ones to help, there will be ones to guide. But you must look around and ask, else how will they know that you require their help? And this is some kind of a metaphor, because of course they would indeed know you need help, but the rules of the game require that you ask, and another may not flood you with assistance, unless by your request, lest they themselves take on the conflict unresolved, that you were experiencing. And this may not be known among your human selves, and that is why when do-gooders try to insist and thrust their help upon another who has not asked, they may find it backfires, it was not welcomed. And they have now involved themselves within the mess.

The world, their world will continue, but it will be at a higher frequency, a higher vibration that does not allow discord and disjointed, dysfunctional patterns of action, and so, from this point it may be deemed another dimension, but to the ones who experience it, it will appear as an ongoing process, a natural occurrence. And to the ones who prefer to stay in turmoil and discord, created by their stubbornness and resistance to change, they shall not miss you. Airheads, they shall think! Fluff heads and pay no more attention to where you went or why. And for those who make their Ascension, it will simply be that such things are no longer a part of their life. So shall it appear, as it is appearing to you now. You are in the corridor, your ascension has begun, and the discord and the turmoil and the fighting is seen as afar. It is not a part of your world. Thus is the Ascension. As you continue along the corridor these things shall fade ever further into the distance, and for you they shall be no more.

I AM Sananda. I AM the Kingdom.
All is within. And the Ascension is the transition
from the old way to the new.
Ascension leads to the inner realms,
to the Kingdom of Peace and Plenty and Purity.
Ascension is the key which allows entrance
to this Kingdom in which you will find
the Ascended Masters, the Angelic Beings,
the Brotherhood of Light, and the Dolphin Ones
in Unity ~ Unity consciousness.

"Our journals are Forcefields of Energy,
Vibration and Consciousness that we enter into
by simply reading and assimilating such Higher Frequencies."
~ Ascended and Free

Thus will it be with Heidi's book!

Ascension Related Concepts

from Whale Wisdom Dolphin Joy
and The Dolphin Ones

In my book *Whale Wisdom Dolphin Joy*, the Cetaceans speak often and eloquently about Enlightenment and Ascension. In the following passage, the Whales give discourse on non-attachment, which they liken to Ascension.

And non-attachment is just that. It is a releasing, a freeing of your frequency, your tonal vibratory rate, not just your desires, foundational beliefs and personal vendettas. Non-attachment is an opening to the vastness of Solar Reality. Non-attachment is the expansion of form. It is a release from the confines and restrictions of a created form. Your form you might see as guidelines to creative living in a manifested world. Think of your body as guidelines to living in a third dimensional world, and the various aches and pains and illnesses are guidelines to those things that you decided to work upon this time around, to release, to let go and grant their own freedom.

The draining emotional ties that you have with others are indications, reminders of the assignment you gave yourself to master and transmute. And as these lessons are completed one by one, and sometimes they may not be totally complete, you do not have to have straight A's to pass the test.

> As long as you reach a certain level,
> a certain grade, a certain frequency,
> you will be free, you will graduate.
> You will Ascend.
> And the ultimate Ascension you see,
> is non-attachment to form.

We are the Archangels who express upon your world as Great Ones of the sea. Silent Watchers in the deep. Guardians of the portals between our worlds. God bless. ~ Transmission Forty-Six, Whales and Archangels on Non-Attachment.

~ ~ ~ ~ ~

Take time each day, or every present moment, to affirm, to know, to clarify your intent for what it is you do, and what you seek, and where it is you go and why. We bless you in your journeys, we swim beside you in your dreams. We hold the concept of Ascension that you hold so dear within your heart, for you ~ beyond the stars. ~ Transmission Twelve, The Dolphins Speak on Clarity of Intent.

~ ~ ~ ~ ~

They (the Dolphins) are the communicators between spirit and matter. And at a subconscious level you know this, and this is one of the reasons why so many of you are drawn to be in the presence of the dolphins. To swim with, to touch and be touched by them at a subconscious level you know they can accelerate your awakening, your return to the I AM Consciousness. Ascension Consciousness, ordained to be realized at this time. ~ Transmission Five, Dolphins as Communicators

~ ~ ~ ~ ~

And we have come as you have come, to hold her (the Earth Star) true, to hold her truth for her as she ascends. As she prepares for her Ascension. And those who ride with her shall fly free too. And there is much to do to ensure that each who wishes to stay with her will not be short circuited, so to speak, by the higher frequencies through which she must pass. ~ Transmission Eight, New Concepts from the Dolphins.

~ ~ ~ ~ ~

It is time for those in your world to unite and call as one to their brethren in the skies, for assistance from the realms of Light. For all is Light no matter what you hear, all is Light. And the darkness is the Light unborn, the Light unlit. But the Light is there, as a tree within its seed. Each may do this individually within their own home, within their own sanctuary, within their own heart they may call. But let each make the same call ~ for the return of Enlightenment.

A cry from the heart for the return of Enlightenment to all who dwell there on. And the unification of this desire shall blaze forth across the nighttime sky and be perceived and honored by those in our realms. And as one, we shall blaze forth from the realms of Unity, Harmony and Balanced Thought, the Rays of Enlightenment to you ones whom we hold so dear. For Enlightenment you see, is a portal to Ascension. ~ Transmission Fifteen, The Dolphin Call to Unite.

~ ~ ~ ~ ~

Enlightenment is a code, a coding embedded deep within your cells, and the sound and sight of this word, this vibration, is a trigger to the memories you hold within ~ that now is a time of assembly, for the coming times. Ascension is a code word too, to which you awaken with joy and excitement. They are interrelated and intertwined, but not synonymous. For Enlightenment is the launching pad of Ascension. Without the launching pad the Ascension could not take place. And without the Ascension ~ for what would you crave the launching pad? ~ Transmission Twenty-One, The Dolphins Speak on Enlightenment.

~ ~ ~ ~ ~

Every cell has at its core a central sun, a starburst of energy, a flame eternal. And it is this zero point to which we refer when we talk about spiritualizing matter. It is the central point or core of matter which shall blaze through its outer trimmings, its outer casing or garments of material manifestation, and seemingly turn these garments inside out. And that which was within shall shine forth in full glory, encapsulating and raising to Enlightenment (Ascension), its former shell. Once again we say, you cannot expect to understand finite things with a mortal mind, it must be grasped in the higher realms and interpreted according to the beliefs and thought system of each. ~ Transmission Thirty, The Dolphins Speak on Cosmic Purpose.

~ ~ ~ ~ ~

As the waves that roll upon the shore give of their life across the sands and withdraw without breaking the motion ~ so should the breath be like this. So should the action of giving and receiving be without halt or break in the motion, in the thought, in the action. This is integration at the highest level. This encompasses all things, which are in truth the Law of Forgiveness in motion.

For all things at this moment
revolve around the point of forgiveness.
And it is on this point of forgiveness
that the Ascension wave shall break,
shall crest and roll in triumph across the land,
the consciousness which it has come to conquer and to rule.

And by conquer and rule, we mean the return of the Christos, Prince of Peace, King of Kings, and Mighty of the mightiest in this land of conscious awareness. ~ Transmission Nineteen, Dolphins and the Point of Integration.

~ ~ ~ ~ ~

This process of Ascension is inevitable. It is simply your choice whether to accept it in full conscious awareness or allow it to seep into your being undetected ~ as one in torpor or drugged state. For so many are in these latter states, unaware. Unconscious almost, of the worlds around and what is available, what choices are available, the options that are to be had. You can help them only by your example. But you cannot force them to walk your path, even though you would take them by the hand and drag them with you on this road to Ascension. You must allow them to follow along at their own pace, and in their own time they shall investigate. But what they do not realize, and what you cannot force them to know is that time is collapsing. They do not have the time they think they have. Structures are falling, and time is a manmade structure, a convenience, and time is collapsing inward upon itself. And the vortex that it creates is the accelerator which intensifies the speed of all particles that serve to hold your world in form.

> And the answer is Light. To fill your bodies,
> your heart, your mind, your thoughts
> and the ways of your world, with Light
> to attain this Enlightenment
> this state of Grace ~ your Ascension.
> ~ Transmission Twenty-Two, The Vortex of Time.

~ ~ ~ ~ ~

Your willingness to dance shall set you free. Free as the ocean waves themselves. Free as the drifting clouds. A freedom shall be yours you have not known for oh, so long, if you will but sing the Song of Upliftment, the Song of Enlightenment, the Song of Ascension, and ride the Waves of Light, that never ever cease to hold you in their sway. We are the Dolphin Ones. We are your Brethren. We are the ones who sing you home this glorious day. ~ Transmission Sixteen, The Dolphin Song of Ascension.

The Dolphin Call to Ascension

Do you hear the Dolphins calling?
Hear their whisper through the air?
Do you hear the Dolphin singing?
Is it pounding in your ear?
'We are the Dolphins calling,
we are the Dolphins you dream.
You are the ones that we hold in our hearts
for we know the same Dream.'

Do you hear the Dolphins calling?
Calling ~ calling to their own?
Secret sacred coded longings, saying,
Home, we're nearly Home.
The Dolphins are calling to their own.
To remember their Lineage.
To recall they are One.
The Dolphins are rising.
The rhythm of Dolphin consciousness
is gathering strength and power.
It calls to those of its kind. It is calling you home.
It is time for the Dolphin People to unite.

Do you hear the Dolphins call?
Do you feel the Dolphin toning sweeping,
wave-like, through your cells?
Does your memory stir and whisper,
'These are your People,
you and the Dolphins are One.'
Not the overall Oneness of All That Is.
But the Oneness of purpose, of a created Lineage.
The Oneness of a lineage created by the One to know Itself.
The Dolphins are calling.
The time of Ascension is upon us.
~ from The Dolphin Ones

Part Three
Animals as Spiritual Beings

Honoring their Divine Nature

This section is a collection of stories and insights in the form of notes and memories of those who came to me or to others, as dogs or cats or horses or whatever ~ as teachers, healers, companions, guides, messengers, caretakers and guardians. Anchors of Goodness and Light and Love. Stories that may bring greater awareness and understanding of the purpose of animals in our lives ~ and of their own purpose, for many animals have their own mission, and accommodating the needs of humans is simply a side effect. And while they are fulfilling their own mission, they may also be demonstrating such qualities as acceptance, surrender, serene detachment and joy, for those who are willing to witness and learn and expand their own spiritual growth and understanding.

The Purpose of Animals in Our Lives

"Many humans find they can interact more easily with 'pets' than they can with other humans. The feline and canine are particularly committed to assisting humans in dealing with isolation, particularly as humans become older and more alone. Both cats and dogs often teach humans to learn to love again, to open their hearts. Dogs are tied to the human emotional field, cats to the human psychic / mental plane. These two very different expressions are both focused on your assistance. Both have the capacity to meld their energy fields with their human and are uniquely capable of becoming personality fragments of their caretakers, and that concise energy can specifically evolve and often reincarnate, or re-attach within other lifetimes, or within the same lifetime, to continue assisting the one known as 'owner'. ~ *James Tyberonn*

The purpose of animals in your life is obvious. We are here to create more love, input and output. An excuse or justification, a reason almost ~ as a means for love to flow. When it does, freely and unconditionally, the role of animals will be complete. ~ The Group (all the little dachshunds speaking as one).

~ ~ ~ ~ ~

Big black Boomer bunny came to stay for a couple of weeks while his family were away. He belonged to a little girl who cuddled him upside down in her arms. He lived in a cage on wheels in my kitchen so I let him out to bounce around the living room two or three times a day. Boomer amazed me with his gentleness, and delightful curiosity to explore and jump up on all and everything. He liked hopping along on top of the couch! He triggered childhood memories in all who met him. I asked Boomer if he would give us comments, words of wisdom that would help me and others understand the seemingly endless boredom of cage confinement. Boomer demonstrated acceptance ~ the Art of Graceful Acceptance.

I surrender to their (his family) needs. I am not in a position to make my own choices, so I just go with the flow. I'm very flexible. I'm part of the family. It's nice to belong somewhere. I can help my family grow. As they know more of my needs their own thought process expands. I'm happy. They love me.

> "Animals do not come into the world
> to learn and experience life as we do.
> They are perfect just the way God made them."
> ~ *Sylvia Browne*

~ ~ ~ ~ ~

I received a photograph of two cats. Bandit and Rubicon. Their person wanted to know why they were in her life, and what was their purpose anyway. I asked who would answer, who would speak.

Well, we are one. We are Star-born and we both came down the same silver shaft. I feel they don't really want to talk about mundane, earthly things. *We don't, we are Star Cats* (I had noticed a flash of light in the photograph), *doing our time on earth.* You mean like time in jail? *No, no, our unit, the group* we are from, always has a certain number or percentage of us on earth at any given time. What do you do? We help balance the energies, maintain the equilibrium, humans are forever upsetting the natural equation with their emotional misunderstandings. We do not dislike our job, we are in acceptance and compassion. We do not dislike our names. Whatever gives our humans pleasure has its effect on us also. Thank you, thank you, thank you. You are welcome. We are Star Cats.

~ ~ ~ ~ ~

Crumpet was an adorable little Cairn Terrier at the local animal shelter. He came in months ago, covered in fleas, itching, and without much hair. Now he is very well, but his forever home seems to be on hold, his adoption does not seem to be a priority, and he continued to spend time shivering in the outside pens. Every day I visit and take him for walkies.

Meanwhile, it is New Year. My Intent is to listen more to the animals. I ask Primrose and Schatzi if they will help me. Seems Primrose will be the speaker, Schatzi indicates that he will speak if there is anything he needs to say. Evidently, I am thinking of Crumpet, because suddenly words flow into my mind. Often they surprise me, I am the witness and have my own thoughts at the comments even as they flow;

Crumpet came to observe. He did not come to suffer. He came to observe, wherever he is. He was not programmed to go to a specific family or for a certain time period. Some dogs are. Crumpet, you would not like the words 'controlled' or 'puppet', so let us just say, Crumpet is an extension of a group soul and in allegiance to that. He enhances the whole. So anything you can do for him adds to the Magnificence of his true Essence. Being cold or lonely or itchy does not detract, it simply is a period where the energies are on hold, motionless in some cases. The energies of progress, growth, evolution, Ascension, whatever word you choose, are stilled. So do not grieve for such as he, wishing and wanting are a waste of your own energies. Rather hold him in the Light, in Joy, in your mind, and do what you can for him, and for those (smile), 'who hold the strings', who are in charge.

Who gives this? It came through Primrose. Primrose has access, a direct line into your heart, so she is currently our liaison, you might say. Who are we? We are The Council of Animals.

Eventually, Crumpet went to a wonderful home where it was planned for him to become a little therapy dog.

Animals can also help us directly if we ask. Candi had an affinity for Beagles, especially those retired or no longer needed as Hunting Beagles. She was having trouble finding a new apartment and the time came when she needed one today! Suddenly she remembered, beagles are hunters! She asked one of her beagles in Spirit to find her a new apartment asap. After a few hours, the telephone rang ~ and Candi had her new apartment!

The Council of Animals Speak

as Representative of the Great Spirit

And as we represent the Great Spirit, so do the Animal Kingdoms represent us ~ the Council of Animals. You may see us as a tree. A Tree of Life. Each Animal Kingdom is a branch of the One. Each twig, each leaf is a subdivision, breed or offshoot of the species. And the fruits of this Tree are their gifts. And the roots of this Tree are their attachment to this Earth, the means by which they are grounded into a manifested reality. And the roots are many, and the fruits are multitudinous, because the Animal Kingdom is Love made manifest, and Love knows no limitation.

And this Tree is watered by the frequency of Divine Grace. This Tree is nurtured by the angels, and fed by the Sun, the Great Central Sun that blazes the Light of Illumination throughout the dimensions, touching the cell, touching the core, the center of each particle that holds this Tree in form ~ allowing the animals creative expression in their Service to the Father's Will. In their Devotion to the Mother's Love.

Honor this Tree, this Tree of Life, and know each animal you touch or see, is an extension of the One, representation of the whole, an expression of the Lord God's Love for you. For each has volunteered to express His Care, to sing Her Song, to be Their Gift. And when you touch their hearts, through word or deed, know that you touch the Heart of your Creator. God bless. We are the Council of Animals ~ the Law of One.

The story about Crumpet being an Observer, reminded me of a previous occasion when I was house sitting two elderly Afghan Hounds. One of them was particularly ancient, and before their people set off on their world travels, they informed me that they had told the veterinarian 'No heroics'. The weather was extremely hot, and although the dogs were household pets and came into the house at night, in the daytime they were left outside in a large paddock with a shed, close to a dirt road with light traffic, and people walking their dogs, and horses in the next field. On the very first day, when I went to bring them indoors, the ancient dog collapsed in a heap at my feet! I phoned the vet, who came immediately, scooped the dog up and took him away saying he was going to give him 24 hours in the air-conditioning before making any decisions. The dog died. That evening, as I sat to meditate, thinking about him ~ I saw his face in front of me. It was his face ~ but with such bright and shining eyes, and it wasn't his face! It was the face of a Wiseman. Or so I thought of the wizened oriental that appeared before me! And I heard the words;

Why the surprise? If a wiseman wanted to experience life on Earth through the eyes of a dog, to know consciousness through the soul of an animal, what better dog to pick? If he had come as a stray, he would have spent all his time hunting for food with no time to observe. And if he had come as a pampered pet, he would have had no interest in paying attention to observing the lives of others. As this dog, he could observe humans and have plenty of time to observe other life around him.

"It can also happen that highly evolved beings enter the body of a certain animal voluntarily in order to study the little-known realm of the animal kingdom." ~ *Omraam Mikhael Aïvanhov*

~ ~ ~ ~ ~

During our Animal Communication Workshops, or Playdays, various exercises were set, usually by the dachshunds ~ Loreli in particular! I had already been given the suggestion to *'consider the evolutionary role of animals in the expansion of human consciousness'.* Loreli evidently thought this was a good idea, and suggested;

Ask them to consider the purpose of animals in their lives. Rather like 'what is the true meaning of Christmas'. We will help them. A thesis on the 'evolutionary role of animals in the expansion of human consciousness'. Not just your own personal lives, but in the lives of humanity. If you would be a true animal communicator you must understand and know the principles with which you work. The ongoing unfoldment of a process that shall lead to transformation of consciousness.

Primrose was the first to answer. *We are teachers. We offer the shy and hesitant, the lonely, angry or bitter, those who would listen to none ~ we offer them ways to love and trust another. We offer ways for them to share their life and space with another living form. We offer ways for them to experience love and maybe laughter. One way or another we come to raise their frequency. To offer hope.*

An answer which reminded me of the magical effect the dogs had on their visits to the elderly in nursing homes, where so often the senior residents had withdrawn into themselves and would talk to no one and participate in nothing. Feeling, watching and being touched by the small furry bodies brought happy smiles, words, and interaction.

> Won't leave his room.
> The rec room? Huh! Too far to walk.
> The wheelchair? Not likely!
> Gretel is tired today, I said.
> But she has things to do and folks to see.
> We placed her in his wheelchair, and leaning on the bar
> he pushed her round on her remaining calls.
> And everyone was pleased.

> *What is it?* A longhaired dachshund.
> *A what?* A longhaired dachshund.
> *I had a dog once ~ long what?* Dachshund.
> *I don't know what they did with it. Here kitty!*
> *Oh, my ~ there's two of them! What are they?*
> They're Gretel and Heidi. Mother and daughter,
> Come in Love, to bring you Joy.

> Festive the hall. The tree was lit. The tables laid.
> The staff assembled. The wheelchairs massed.
> It was too much.

Back to his room, in solitude he lay.
The speechmaker. And now alone.
Unfulfilled. Discouraged.
The head nurse told me. Would Gretel visit him?
I knocked. He was polite.
Useless words. Despair prevailed.
I lifted Gretel to his side.
She lay beside him, knowing this was silly.
Motionless, I watched her as she climbed across his chest
and nestled 'neath his good right arm.
An arm that moved to hold her.
She sighed and snuggled close.
Smiling through love filled eyes
they touched each other's soul.
And in the Silence, healing came.
I had not known ~ his other arm was paralyzed.

~ ~ ~ ~ ~

And then, I had an amazing connection with a horse, one of several in the paddock, and this one came up to the fence. I thanked him for allowing me to pet him, and asked wordlessly and without much intent, what is your purpose, why did you come? *Those were my orders.* It took a few seconds to realize what he had said. And a couple more to integrate the depth and profundity of this remark, these four words ~ those were my orders. Love, Serve and Obey came to mind. How many of us can do this? I have met more than one ex monk who said, I could do everything except obey. And yet this horse, and how many other animals, willingly obeyed his Orders.

Who is he? To what Order does he belong? Who gave the orders? This horse had no doubt he was Serving Love and goes where Love commands. To planet Earth as a horse, where he is gentle, kind and patient. Horses do not always stay with one 'owner', or in one place, but he has surrendered his own needs to Serve in Love, wherever he is needed. And if his departure from this dimension is not gentle and kind, it is not a concern for him. It is part of his acceptance of the Plan which called for his presence here at this time.

~ ~ ~ ~ ~

Shelly phoned. Her 13-year-old cat had what might have been a stroke the previous night and had just passed away at the veterinary clinic. She wanted Springer to know how much she loved her, and that she wanted to continue to be with her. Was she O.K?

I sat outdoors between the pine trees on my sheepskin mat and invited Springer to join me. I wondered if she would mind the little dachshunds who were also sitting with me and made sure there was room for her between us. But no Springer came. I could get no sense of her presence or form. I continued asking my questions anyway, and eventually words flowed into my mind;

It was my time, need more be said? And because I am a Master Cat was it given to me to choose my death, my exit, my style of transition. You cannot see me because it is not necessary for me to hold the cat form longer, I am as I said, a Master. If Shelly will look back upon her life, she will see that during all major crises, all major decisions or deviations from the norm, what humans think of as crisis, major decisions and deviations from the norm that is, I was there. Springer the Master Cat was there to support and nurture her.

And then there comes a time when change is ordered and growth expected. And I am here to support and nurture that growth, but in a different aspect, a different form, another variation of the norm. I am her guide. Her teacher I remain. To say that she loves her cat Springer, and that Springer returns these emotions are words in action, as your hand caressing your dog is an expression of your love in action. Neither are ever wasted; each is a part of the whole.

Know that I AM with you and shall ever be a part of your very existence, for I AM far more than Springer cat, guide or teacher. I am a part of your very Self made manifest, as a gem to treasure always in your heart. Remember me with love (meaning, remember only the happy times). And when times are such that cause you feelings of dismay or gloom, think upon Springer Cat, and know that you are ever loved in Truth, as you and she expressed on Earth.

~ ~ ~ ~ ~

Although the focus here seems to be on our household pets and domesticated animals, these concepts may apply to all animals. I was stunned one day when standing on a street corner outside Jerusalem to find myself beside a seated camel. Awed to be so close to such a magnificent animal, I contemplated deeply on the possibility of actually touching it. Nobody was in sight, and the camel seemed agreeable, so I reached out to gently stroke its neck ~ as soon as my fingers touched its hair, I knew ~ waves of awareness flowed through me. That here was an angelic being, part of a band of angels who voluntarily came to Earth in Service, to help humanity in their process of evolution, their return to Wholeness, to Oneness. To carry their burdens, to provide nourishment and shelter. *To be carriers of Light.* That as they trekked across the deserts in silent Service, they would *also be anchoring the Light of a Thousand Suns* with each softly padded footfall across the Earth. They also they came with the understanding that all Life is Sacred ~ including their own.

An understanding or original pact I believe was expected by all animals, all Elementals, which includes the unseens, the nature spirits, gnomes and fairies, who dwell within and upon our planet. And I was reminded of the time a friend asked me; What is the relationship between a horse and its person? I took the answer to be valid for all animals.

It is a Sacred Trust. The animal comes in trust that it will be honored and taken care of. Not necessarily loved but treated with respect. For all Life is One, and in the acknowledgment of this, the caretaker, guardian, companion or whoever ~ honors their own life, the essence or spirit of that life, that consciousness.

~ ~ ~ ~ ~

And then one day when I was hiking along the silent unmarked trails of the Holy Land, I came across a herd of cattle, calm and serene, peacefully resting together 'in the middle of nowhere'. Chewing their cud and dreaming the day away! And I understood they were 'holders of the Light'. That their presence, and the presence of other herds or flocks of animals like them, was of great importance towards helping maintain the frequency of balance and harmony in a volatile area. For even in those days (1971), peace was never ensured.

Animals as Teachers and Healers

Their wisdom, compassion and advice

I called to those in Spirit to come and give me words regarding animals as Teachers and Healers. I played a tape of Indian flute music which started with a haunting refrain called Song of the Wolf, and the following words flowed instantly through my mind:

Since time began animals have been honored and recognized as teachers and healers. Guides and way showers through the spirit kingdoms. The wisdom of their group consciousness has been sought by Indigenous peoples who respected this wisdom, who sought their answers, their teachings. And gradually now, ones are awakening to this fact, expanding their consciousness, their beliefs to include what other life forms have to give, to offer, and to share.

As a healing balm for emotions, contact with the animal kingdoms has no equal. Therapeutically they offer peace and calming, just by their presence, whether it be fish swimming in a tank at the doctor's office, the contemplation of birds and bees on a summer's day, or the nearness and dearness of a beloved pet. And to actually touch, to pet, to hold this animal is to greatly reduce the stresses that are experienced by ones in mental conflict with their self and with each other.

Long has man watched and tried to emulate the way of the animal kingdoms, and here we would include the birds and insects, all life other than human ~ in the building of their homes. Long have they pondered how it is the animals know the changing of the seasons, impending storms and earthquakes. And now there are many who are opening to the possibilities, the probabilities, of communicating with these voiceless wordless beings who share their planet and appear so very much in tune with each other and their surroundings.

And they are discovering, these ones who would open to such communications, that there is a level of depth and understanding available but for the asking. To align one's intent with the rhythm of an animal is rather like entering a portal into another dimension, to receive the wisdom of a higher frequency or level of understanding.

And the hearts of the ones who would know are opened through love for their animal brethren, their animal kin. And unconditional love for the animals will lead eventually to acceptance and love for their human family. But until they can feel this love at a heart level, it will be hard to communicate at the telepathic level of which we speak.

If you will take the time to still your mind and open your heart, you will find that your animals can offer great insights and hope, understanding and philosophical truths ~ if you will but ask, and give them time to reply.

And when we speak of animals as healers, we speak of healing the mind where the misconceptions originate. A closeness and oneness with the animals will lower the resistance to do battle against another, to do battle against yourself.

The qualities that so many admire in their beloved pets are but reflections of their own inner beauty, mirrored to them by these teachers in silence. They out picture for us the joy that our Creator intended ever to be ours. They reflect for us our state of mind and the condition of the world we create around us ~ if we would but take the time to notice and observe. They come in gentleness, they come in grace. And how we perceive their actions is ever a commentary upon our own level of understanding.

Some may note only the ferocity with which a daily meal is prepared, others will see only the tenderness in sharing this meal with mate or young, and wonder ~ and open to receive divine insights. Another will close with disgust. One quickens their vibratory rate through appreciation and awe. The other lowers their frequency with a display of negative emotions.

The choice of perception is yours, oh dearly beloveds. And we would say, we would suggest, that if there is something on any front that bothers you, that you do not understand ~ that you ask the spirit, the essence of the animal or animals involved, to show you a higher perspective, an expanded viewpoint, a greater understanding, and be prepared for sudden and spontaneous insights. For great ah-ha's.

Is each and every animal a teacher, a healer? We would say, within each one is the potential for such. If the need is present the potential will surface. But those who choose to remain unaware will see nothing, feel nothing, until they choose to expand the borders of their world to include all life. Until they choose to live as much as possible by the decree of Reverence for Life. God bless, we are the Council of Animals, and the angels who work through your animals, and the Spirit of Francis of Assisi. A conglomeration of apparent and forgotten outcasts who would be heard through the medium of an open heart and speak ever in accordance with your own High Self. God bless.

~ ~ ~ ~ ~

This reminded me of one of our Animal Communication Playdays here at Sananda. Participants are requested to bring a photo of an animal they know well. An exercise is set for them to choose a photo, converse with the animal, and then get feedback from the animal's person. On this occasion, there were four photos left for me to choose from, all animals that had already been 'talked with', so I asked all four of them to speak as one. Spirit, Peanut, Jake and Smuckers. Three small elderly dogs and one middle aged cat. Do you understand what we're doing? I asked.

Yes, this is a learning forum for people. You are learning what we know. We are the teachers. Teaching you how to remember. To have faith in yourselves. To credit the abilities that you cannot see, that are innate to all. We are to help you develop your birthright. Bring us your problems and worries and insecurities, we can help. But also bring us your joy and fun, we can help you lighten up. The Elders have spoken.

~ ~ ~ ~ ~

Friend Sharon wrote; Cleo my cat died on Thursday. She was eleven. Cleo suffered a sudden, vicious, out of nowhere attack by two strange dogs. You will have to tell me where she went. She was my teacher of forgiveness. A treasure for sure.

So I asked. Where did Cleo go? And immediately I heard; *She went into the Silence. Just as Primrose came from Love, so Cleo came from the Great Great Silence, and unto THAT she has returned.* Maybe it's the same thing? I sat to meditate. What is the difference between Love and Silence? And the thought came; *Love and Wisdom, Christ and Buddha. They are One and the same, only the limitations of a human mind cause the appearance of difference or separation.* And I thought of Temple cats, the Mother Essence of Temple cats. The soul frequency of the group ~ it was as an emanation or breath of this that came to Sharon.

A single breath of Love and Compassion that came to assist Humanity through one person. A dedicated lineage, for in this dimension one must dress and play by the rules of that existence. As Primrose came in Love, from Love, in accordance with the frequency of Love ~ so did Cleo play the game according to the rules, and embodied the frequency of Compassion, a more refined frequency than that of Forgiveness. That is her Teaching. Compassion for the One, for the All, for the self. Compassion for the self. Which all must learn. Sooner or later. Willing or not. Love is contained within the Silence, and one cannot enter the Silence without passing through Love. They are one, merged and blended, in seeming separation only to pass more easily through the minds and understanding of a lesser frequency. Cleo and Primrose flow through one another as the inbreath and the outbreath. Each meaningless without the other:

> Love exists in Silence. And Silence cannot Be without Love.
> How the poor little human does struggle to comprehend!
> Allow! Accept! And know ~ this is.
> Silence waits for Love. Love in Silence waits.
> While Truth and Beauty flow in Grace,
> Creative Grace that flows forever through Love's Silence.
> And in the Silence of a Radiant Heart at Peace ~ Love knew herself.

~ ~ ~ ~ ~

So often the animals share their compassion through forgiveness, showing the needless foolishness of worry and guilt. I thought of the time friend Mary, with tears in her eyes, told of her old black racehorse, Shadow. She loved him so much, he was so gentle. She felt a great bond, a real love between them. Shadow had died painfully of colic when she was only twelve years old. Now she was midlife, and still felt she had failed him. Guilty that she had not with him when he died. She was at school! She wanted me to tell him that she loved him, and to ask if there was anything she needed or could do for him.

I figured I had better change the Temple setting (the Temple in my mind), to one more appropriate for a horse. It had been a comfortable room with plush and snuggly armchairs appropriate for an elderly cat the last time I was in it. But already, before I could call to him, a gorgeous black horse was racing across open grassland towards me. Mane flowing in the breeze, head tossing, blowing through his nostrils. Playfully he came to a halt in front of me. I put out my hand to touch his muzzle. Gently, gently, he tried to avoid my hand and nuzzle my face. I began to tell him how much Mary loved him; *I know. I know.* He was Christ like in his understanding and gentleness. She feels she fails you, I continued. He blew through his nostrils with a small shake of his head.

I have come galloping up from her past, over the rocks and gullies. Across sweet meadows and beautiful rivers (in my mind, I saw him doing this ~ scrambling up slippery banks and crossing desert lands). *I have raced through Time to stand here now, so she may heal her past and know I live, am strong. A spirit horse with eagle wings. No more the earth for me. For I have found my freedom in the fields of Heaven, and race the winds of Time for fun, for joy. And I shall take her through the outer realms of space if she would wish. Just call my name. Call Shadow, and I shall be beside her in my dream. And she may climb upon my back, and I shall show her marvels beyond the dream she thinks is hers. She may share My Dream if she would wish.*

Mary could only stare at the words on the paper I handed her; "That's how my whole life has been," she whispered. "Rocks and gullies and meadows and rivers."

"The spiritual growth of animals I believe and know, is inextricably linked to ours as humans. I see the extraordinary role they are playing at the moment, helping people to open their hearts, and bring comfort, joy, humor and all the other wonderful things they bring to us. All life is ascending to a higher state of consciousness." ~ *Anthea Torr*

~ ~ ~ ~ ~

I will never forget the totally unexpected compassion shown to me by Marshall, a Shetland Sheepdog. Candace, my last little dachshund had recently died, and I was visiting my elderly neighbor. A year or so earlier, five-year-old Marshall had come to live with her. A kennel dog, a stud dog, totally unsocialized to humans. As so often happens with such animals, he bonded immediately with his 'rescuer', and would have nothing to do with anyone else. He had previously slipped his collar and run away from me when I tried to take him for a walk! But he did know me, and he knew Candace. Lilian and I were sitting opposite each other at her dining room table when I felt Marshall's nose touch my knee. I told Lilian what just happened. We could only stare at each other in wonder. Marshall was offering his condolences. How did he know? Normally he would not voluntarily come anywhere near me.

"How is it that animals understand things I do not know, but it is certain that they do. Perhaps there is a language which is not made of words, and everything understands it? Perhaps there is a Soul hidden in everything and it can always speak, without even making a sound." ~ A Little Princess

~ ~ ~ ~ ~

The following teaching, or advice, was given as a rather stern lecture to a young lady headed to college and who was desperately, and seemingly rather unreasonably, trying to control what became of her beloved horses.

Those that come as domestic house pets usually come to one specific person and are often aspects of their own High Self, their Twin Angel or Master Teacher. And those that come in form that are not quite so personal, that must live outside the dwelling space, have often come with double, triple, or even multiple projects or goals, intentions and undertakings. And as each is completed, or nears completion, they must move on, move elsewhere for their next assignment, and it is not for you, for the former chela of these Great Ones to 'hang on' and try to manipulate their destinies, their future. It is for you to hold the Light for them, to invoke their highest and greatest good, in accordance with the highest and greatest good for all, yourself included. ~ The Group

~ ~ ~ ~ ~

The animals, it seemed, could answer any question we could conceive of. So often we are told or given phrases encouraging us to 'just be here now', or to 'stay in the present moment.' Candace was sitting on my lap and the thought occurred to ask the dogs for insights on this. Or rather the Animal Kingdoms. What does this mean to you, I asked? And how can we apply it in our own lives?

For us, Being in the Present Moment is the ability, the desire to have all our senses tuned to the needs of the Present Moment. How we are experiencing ourselves, our surroundings, the Life Force itself, in the Now time. Being in the Now gives no power to the past or future, no diversification of our intent, our purpose. Our purpose, our very reason for Being, is to know and experience this Gift of Life in physical embodiment to maximum potential, and this can only be accomplished in the Present Moment. All else is deviation from this Truth, a distraction formulated by the lower self or ego mind.

Claim your Power, O Humans and Be Here Now! When distractions occur and the mind wanders, focus on the Breath, the Breath of Life ~ for that is the constant that never wavers. The Breath of Life is ever present and ever available. It is your choice where to Be. Where your consciousness shall Be. ~ Ah-ho and God bless, the Animal Kingdoms.

But on another occasion, when I was in the presence of a newborn foal and thought to ask her what she might have to say about 'just being here now', in her new existence, I was told;

She has not yet truly separated her thoughts from the One. She comes from the depths of Oneness into diversity. Give her time. The wild ones, those unrelated to human influence remain ever in touch with their Source, the One. Those born into human domain are often overwhelmed, or at least affected by and must adjust to or merge with their family unit on earth. In other words, their thoughts and behavior reflect in part, their surroundings, and she needs time to explore this reality.

Communicating with Animals

Are we communicating or communing? Communicating is perhaps most often thought of as an exchange of ideas, thoughts, information. Communing may be more subtle, including feeling and sensing, a wordless experience, as in 'communing with Nature'. Perhaps there is no real dividing line, perhaps these concepts blend and merge and work together as one.

Communion, by our standards, is the heart connection, the feeling aspect of Oneness. Communion is received in silence. It is knowing, and if you wish for words, then you must formulate them from what you feel within your heart. Communion is when you know and when you feel without hearing or seeing, it is a resonance. It could be said to be that instant when two hearts beat as one. When you are suffused with love and filled with emotion, that is communion. ~ God bless, we are the Dolphin Ones, Master Communicators, perfected in the art of resonance.

"To commune is to enter into relationship with all creatures, and with the living force which animates rocks, plants, mountains, springs, the sun and the stars. Those who truly know how to commune are able by their love and wisdom to establish contact with all creatures in the universe."
~ Omraam Mikhaël Aïvanhov

"Many people talk to their animals.
Not many listen though.
That's the problem." ~ Winnie the Pooh

A couple of examples that the animals really can and do hear us: Gretel didn't go to the vet very often, but when she did, she would start shaking and trembling as soon as we got out of the car and headed for the clinic door. So! I had been reading about animal communication! And decided the next time her teeth needed cleaning, I would tell her what was going to happen. I would start explaining to her three days ahead of time what to expect and that it was no big deal, that she would just be there a short time, and I would come and take her home, etc., etc. She understood alright, she shook so hard for three days straight, and her teeth chattered and rattled so much I was afraid there might none left to clean!

The week before Lorna joined us, every evening in my meditations, I would send her silent invitations to come and explore the house, and to join us in bed at night if she wished. Her breeder and friend eventually delivered her to the door, and after a bit of garden time, we all came inside. Phyllis and her friend sat on the couch and Lorna walked on past them and into the kitchen where we could all hear her having a nice drink. After a stunned silence, one of them murmured, how did she know where the water was? Oh! said I, she's been coming here every night!

As for Heidi, if and when she wanted out in the middle of the night, instead of standing at the door waiting for her to come back, I could just tell her to bark when she was ready. Heidi and I had such a profound and special rapport that I could actually go back to sleep, knowing that she would not only bark, but that she could also silently alert me, wake me up, when she was at the door and ready to come in. No way could I or would I have done that with any of the other dogs.

I would also add that many of us have fine examples that our animals can and do hear us and our requests ~ and do as they please anyway!

Oneness, the Unity of Life ~ knowledge of which may be achieved through communication. Communicating at the heart level where all is one. All living things, all Life has a heartbeat, a pulsation, a certain tone or vibratory rate, a frequency that may be known as a sound. And it is with this sound that we would have ones communicate, connect at a heart level with the sound of another. And the sound of each may be interpreted according to the language of the one who speaks. And the one who speaks may speak in silence, in thoughts, in words or pictures, within their mind ~ translated as a knowingness. For the intent that lies behind the words is the knowingness that goes forth. And there is a transducer between the communicator and the communicatee.

And that transducer is in the Heart of the Great Central Sun,
and its Rays project through all Life.
Invisible Rays of a frequency and pitch so high,
so fine, so pure that none may touch or see,
and few may feel or know.
Be clear, be pure, and know that this is Truth.
God bless ~ We are the Brotherhood of the Sun,
the Great Central Sun, who come to you this day
in celebration of your acceptance of our words.

~ ~ ~ ~ ~

And then there are what I call spontaneous exchanges. Situations where I might ask a question but don't really expect a response, or it 'just happens' anyway. It was January, and I accidentally came across a large fat toad hibernating in the flower bed. We both scared each other. I had tried to move him, I thought he was a stone! I apologized and asked him how he felt about being woken so abruptly, but he said *oh, just go away!*

Another time, I was taking the first Spring hike in the nearby State Park when I met another fine toad sitting in the middle of the trail. I picked him up, told him what a fine fellow he was, kissed him on the nose, told him he was my Prince Charming and set him back on the ground saying happily; There! How do you feel now?! He said he felt as though he had just been abducted by an alien!

And on my morning walk, one cold and sunless winter's morn, I passed a herd of cattle and noticed, out in the middle of the snowy field, a small newborn calf leaping and bouncing around. Oh! I said in my mind, you are being so adorable! Immediately he responded, *I'm not being adorable, I'm trying to get warm!*

And then there was the fly! A huge, healthy, irritating fly. It was the middle of winter so I couldn't leave the doors and windows open. I made several useless efforts to catch and release, and by the third day, was so exasperated, I exclaimed ~ what are you doing in here anyway?! Clearly, promptly, I heard, *I'm a house fly*. This made me laugh! Caused a change in attitude, and the fly didn't seem to bother me anymore. Once we relinquish attack mode, the 'enemy' ceases to exist.

And then I met a very special cat. I was staying with new friends in Maui ~ and their beautiful long-haired tabby called Mademoiselle. Her people were also very special, gentle and kind. I could see that Rose had a very special bond with this feline, and when Mademoiselle came to visit me in my little room, unthinkingly I asked her something like who was she anyway! *I'm a Zen cat,* she said. Rose was overcome with delight! I hadn't known about her deeply spiritual nature and that she helped Ram Dass with his daily chores.

And my friend Renee, who was sitting on the couch with one of her five cats who was methodically massaging her chest, asked; What are you doing?! *I'm pushing Goodness into you,* responded Mei Ling.

"A cat purrs to affect the vibratory pattern around her. You can hear her contributions to life and know that she is emanating soothing efforts of thought and feeling. Her thoughts and feelings are not as complex as those of humans, in that she stays very much focused on what she is doing. She is emanating a vibratory ray that is soothing and love filled. She hums the song of the universe, like a lullaby that is calming in its simplicity. She is contributing to the enlightenment of the Earth." ~ *Joan Norton*

> "Clearly animals know more than we think,
> and think a great deal more than we know."
> ~ Dr Irene M. Pepperberg Ph.D.

Transition

Inevitably there comes a time for discussion on animals in our past, and the grief and guilt so often still involved. Grief and guilt that the animals seem to indicate is rather an unnecessary waste of time and energy.

Thomas was a beautiful grey cat who had left his earthly body in a bit of a mess. Although this had happened many years ago, Rebecca still grieved for him, and feared that he died a traumatic death. She wanted to know where is he? How does he feel? What is doing? I asked for words that would set her heart at ease. And Thomas gave me a picture of himself ~ he had been lying on his back, and suddenly he squiggled, wiggled sideways, sort of turned himself in a half-moon and rolled over peering up at me. He says he enjoys doing that, because he feels he is a very athletic kind of cat, and he enjoys stretching and feeling the flexibility of his muscles and his legs, and he says;

Oh, it wasn't so traumatic you know. The transition might have been a little bumpy perhaps, but I can handle it. No worse than anybody taking a small boat ride and feeling a little seasick. The boat gets you where you're going, doesn't it? So it doesn't matter if you don't feel so good while it's happening. But my most important priority, the only thing I really wanted to do, was to be where they could find me, so they would know what happened. So that they would know, and not spend much time looking for me and wondering where did he go? That would have left her heart in torment, I do know. And so I did what I wanted to do most, parked my body where they would find it, and then I was free to leave, to go, to fly. I had completed my mission. I didn't want to hang around and be an old cat, die of diseases, get stuffed full of medicines, oh, no! I am a free cat. I am a fast cat. I am a slinky-linky-dinky do cat! And Thomas was a very good name for me, it added a little dignity I feel, to my presence.

And now, what do I do now? I roam. I roam the fields of Starlight; the universe is my home. I travel the moonbeams, the star lines. I know a freedom and expansion that I never knew on Earth. And yet it was important that I came, to complete my education, in a way. For I am a Master Cat. And I have many credits to my name, and now I can add the title 'x resident of Earth'. 'Observer and calculator of humanity and human ways'. 'Experienced pet, and hunter of physical things'.

Oh, my life was a grand success, I think. And I liked my humans very much. I did not know or expect that I would enjoy them so much. But I did. And I would send that little one who played with me (Rebecca was a child at the time), Star blessings and moonbeam caresses. I am a Star cat, and the universe is my home.

~ ~ ~ ~ ~

The actual transition, which may be pretty traumatic for us, may be the equivalent of an epiphany for the animal. I had been trying to help support a friend via telephone conversations, whose beloved horse was dying. Much suffering was involved, but the vet could do nothing more and she was not about to have the horse euthanized. Saturday morning came, a dreary day with overcast sky. They were all outside in the paddock. Suddenly, the dying horse was on full alert. Standing tall, he neighed loudly, whirled around, and dropped dead. All in the same instant, the sky turned black, the thunder rolled, and the sun burst through the clouds causing a wild display of brilliant color in all directions. More like a dramatic sunset than 10 am in the morning.

I was given to understand that this horse was a great soul who was able to open a portal at his passing, allowing the release of many animals and humans who were 'stuck' or 'on hold', taking them with him in his transition ~ in his Ascension. I also felt that that the great suffering this horse endured and transcended had something to do with enabling or allowing for the opening of this portal.

A few years later, I was in Colorado. Out in the pasture, a young two-year-old filly appeared in great distress. Very slowly, we were able to bring her into the barn. Veterinarians were few and far between, but her person went off to the house and telephone to see what she could do. I stayed with the horse. Pretty soon she collapsed and lay stretched out and quivering on the ground, obviously beyond help. I was about to leave her and suggest cancelling the veterinarian ~ when she scrambled to her feet, stood tall and strong, gazing eagerly, with shining eyes and perked ears, through the barn walls towards the East at something only she could see. She neighed powerfully, long and loud ~ and dropped dead. The other horses, her companions, were not in that direction at all.

And then Frosty, a child's elderly pet pony died. We gathered for a meditation to send Frosty our love. A group of five children and three adults, sitting on my carpeted living room floor. I offered a little guided visualization to invite Frosty to join us and asked if he would give each child some comforting thoughts or words that would bring them peace. He did indeed come to each, and everyone radiated big smiles and happy Frosty stories! As for me ~ he had taken me for a ride on his back, but he was huge and vast, and I lay seemingly small and insignificant in the dip of his back, holding on to his mane and peering down over his shoulder as we flew across the land. For some reason, we were passing over the entire country, and I watched his shadow on the earth below. But it was not the shadow of a small pony ~ *it was the shadow of a great angel.*

~ ~ ~ ~ ~

All of which led to asking Lorna to tell us about Love, from her perspective; *There must be love. Love of and for oneself. It's all very well to open the heart, but if you are not in harmony and at peace with yourself this input can be too great for the heart to handle, and it may shatter and fragment. 'I love this dog. I love this cat. I love all animals so much it hurts.' Dear ones, know that if you can love yourself too, as we love you, you can love us even more because it won't hurt. And you won't be afraid of losing our love.*

Love is born to flow, to express,
to share of itself ~ to merge and blend,
becoming one with the Love of another.

"To love and be loved, to give and receive love ~ this is what human beings need more than anything. And the truth is, that their need to love is even greater than their need to be loved. It is only our love for others that stimulates and inspires us; it is the greatest source of blessings. This is why you must never prevent your heart from loving. Never stop loving all creation and all creatures, and at the same time always seek the best way to express your love." ~ *Omraam Mikhaël Aïvanhov*

*Bearers of Light ~ Teachers of Love.
The animals come to awaken Compassion.
They come to help us know Compassion,
and Reverence for Life.*

~ ~ ~ ~ ~

And then a friend phoned concerning Fat Boy, a wild cat she had spent five years trying to catch. Finally she did, and he had to be kept in a cage for months, so wild he was. Eventually, one day when she was feeding him, her arm in the cage, he dropped his head upon her hand and became the most affectionate and loving cat they ever had. He slept on their bed. And now, Fat Boy had woken in the night to use his litter box, and on the way back he paused, looked them straight in the eye, and gently crumpled to the floor, his spirit released from form.

Was there a particular reason for his exit in this manner? Was it his heart? I invited the cat to speak ~ silently, immediately, I heard him say;

It was not my heart. It had nothing to do with my heart. Of course, there was a reason for my departure in this manner. It caught their attention did it not? And will they not tell this story to many? And will this not sow seeds, of how the transition from one dimension to another may be made in peace, through grace, without fuss and bother. And each one that passes in this manner, makes it easier for the others to follow. It is what you would call the hundredth monkey effect in action, being built even as you watch. The possibility that this is so is being created in the minds of all who hear such stories.

And you will hear more as you share them. It will trigger others to share their own experiences and witness for themselves how it is done. Yes indeed, they shall witness others do as I have done. I am a forerunner. I am a Wayshower. I am a trail blazer. And indeed other animals in my so called predicament of wildness shall be quickened in their surrender because I passed before. It was the same principle. What one has done another may do, and another, and another, and another. And the way in which they do it is speeded up each time. As I am lifted up, all life is lifted with me ~ in other words, once the trail has been cut, the others may pass more swiftly.

~ ~ ~ ~ ~

We understand your reluctance to part with the physical forms of your beloveds. But we say to you, each time one leaves it is their wish that human minds will open to encompass their new reality, rather than close and experience loss. Each time one leaves you, take it as an opportunity to practice expansion of the mind. Expansion of your understanding of reality. And tell to as many as will listen the results of your experience. God bless ~ We are the Council of Animals who come in reverence for one who cares for so many of our Tribe.

~ ~ ~ ~ ~

"They (dogs and cats) are not on Earth to evolve.
They are already evolved.
They are here on Earth to support the Earth,
and assist mankind in so doing,
as companions, healers and protectors."
~ James Tyberonn

~ ~ ~ ~ ~

As consciousness-raising continues, people will learn that the souls of animals evolve, and that they deserve the same care and respect as humans. Some animals, usually those who are pets, are aspects of human souls who chose to experience in an animal body, and even when this isn't the case, they have emotional and characteristic ranges similar to those of humans ~ lacking only acquired traits such as tact, deception and wiliness.

"The higher orders of animals need to give and receive love as much as humans, and in many cases do so more readily and loyally. Even those in the lower orders form bonds with people who tend to their needs. Including your pets in meditations and energy therapy is uplifting to them in their awareness of your recognizing their true selves. When we say that every soul is a part of God and all souls are One, this includes animals!" ~ Matthew

Blessed Is the Heart

from the Sanskrit

Blessed is the Heart
that can pierce through appearance and find Truth.
Clear is the spiritual aura
of one who needs only touch the fringe of Godliness,
and in humility bow before the Grace of the Holy Spirit.
Pray always that when the spirit of Truth comes among you,
you may be among the first to kneel in adoration before its Flame.
Wiser than the greatest seer in the kingdom
is the one who can pierce through the garments of flesh
and salute the pure God.

The one who lives true to all Life,
has senses constantly sharpened to hear the Voice of Life
that may emanate from any person,
any tree, bush or bird that flies,
according to the spirit of God
who may want to speak with that person
at various times, for the good of the whole.
Be alert ever, for the Homeland
is constantly endeavoring to reach you,
and wise is the one who is ever attuned
to its Celestial Song.

Acknowledgements

Thanks and Gratitude to the Following for Comments and Permission to Quote from their Works

Ascended and Free ~ for permission to quote copiously from their monthly journals. Best described (in part) by their Victory Statement: "Ascended and Free, Together, standing in the Light! Ascended and Free is a Forcefield of Divine Consciousness which provides a Sacred Template, an outline for individual and group Lightwork. By energizing and anchoring the Theme of each month, we unify into a global service." ~ AscendedAndFree.org

Dr J. J. and Dr Desiree Hurtak ~ authors, social scientists, futurists and founder of the Academy For Future Science, for permission to quote from The Gospel of Mary. ~ FutureScience.org ~ KeysOfEnoch.org

Hay House, Inc. ~ founded in 1984 by author Louise Hay, for permission to quote from Anna, Grandmother of Jesus by Claire Heartsong, first published in 2002. ~ HayHouse.com

Patricia Cota-Robles ~ spiritual teacher. Co-founder of the nonprofit organization Era of Peace, and New Age Study of Humanity's Purpose, Inc. ~ EraOfPeace.org

Prosveta ~ an independent publishing house dedicated to distributing the many teachings of the Bulgarian spiritual Master Omraam Mikhaël Aïvanhov (1900 – 1986), whose own spiritual Master, Peter Deunov, sent to France in 1937 to spread the ideals of transforming ourselves and the whole world into a space of beauty, peace, love, light, and purity. The spiritual community, Le Bonfin that Aïvanhov founded in the south of France is still strong and active today. ~ Prosveta-USA.com

William Henry ~ who said Heidi was Light slowed down! Author and authority on our spiritual potential, transformation, and ascension. Frequently seen on Ancient Aliens. ~ WilliamHenry.net

Matthew ~ regularly channels information to enlighten, encourage and guide us on our ascension journey, through his mother Suzanne. ~ MatthewBooks.com

Peter Deunov (Beinso Douno 1864 - 1944) ~ Bulgarian spiritual Teacher, master musician (violin) and composer of sacred music, who spoke often of the coming new era. The birthing of a new consciousness based on Love, Wisdom and Truth. He gave us the joyful and meditational 'dance' of Paneurhythmy which we do here in the Garden of Sananda, the movements and meaning of which contain the essence of his teachings. He spoke on just about every subject imaginable, from family and nutrition to worlds beyond. He taught that the greatest achievement for a human being ~ is to love every living creature.

Dan Winter ~ physicist, electrical engineer, and way beyond, speaks of 'direct transmissions of Light taken to God Consciousness'. On hearing the Heidi story, said, Heidi was the perfect wave! ~ FractalField.com

Ingrid ~ Rev. Ingrid Joly, intuitive teacher of Cosmic Truths. ~ Avillion.org

Anthea Torr ~ offers a wealth of Ascension related information from the Ascended Masters. ~ IAmFree.co.za

Sananda Ascension Essences

32 Vibrational flower and mineral infusions from the Garden of Sananda

I include mention of the Sananda Ascension Essences because there is reference to them in this book, and because the little dogs so loved the Playdays when people came to learn how to make their own! Briefly, flower essences are made by floating them in a glass bowl of water in the morning sunlight, and by invoking assistance from the nature spirits and assorted Beings of Light. Coupled with our intent, the flowers release and imprint their qualities into the water which retains the memory. After a brief time of stabilization, we put this water into little dropper bottles, usually with a very small amount of brandy as holding agent, and take as needed – traditionally, a drop or two under the tongue.

The little dogs loved all parts of this Playday ceremony! Especially they loved the picnic lunch break! And then, during the discussion on 'what the fairies said', and how people had been guided to find their flower, the little dogs would nonchalantly wander away on their own little investigations, which usually included sampling the water in the prior mentioned bowls! The water is supposed to remain pure and uncontaminated, but everyone seemingly felt honored and delighted if their bowl was chosen by a little dachshund for tasting! On one occasion, Candace actually ate all the flowers in the bowl! The water had already been bottled, but Melissa had set the flowers aside to take home to her mother ~ and Candace ate them! Another participant gallantly relinquished her own flowers for Melissa to take home. The flowers have actually had their stems removed, but they are always so pretty floating on the water.

Sometimes described as liquid homeopathic remedies, flower and mineral essences can help us change our perspective, our way of thinking and acting, enabling our beliefs to expand, our emotions to dissipate and the Truth of our Being to shine through! By transmuting or dissolving the related emotion causing pain or tensions, there may also be a release or lightening in the physical body. Essences offer support to our personal growth and inner knowing. They quicken and transform the past by accelerating our vibratory rate, activating sacred codings within the inner template of our being ~ creatively renewing our lives! They help us reclaim our Power and Sovereignty, to live our lives in joy and gladness. They offer vibrational upliftment and fast forward our consciousness into living and being our highest potential ~ our Ascension into Light!

Flower Essences are an excellent support to any therapeutic or spiritual work. It is our personal need that dictates which one to use. Make your choice, affirm your intent, and place a drop or two under the tongue. They may also be placed in a bowl of water and offered to any situation, condition or thing, and/or gifted to the Earth, the oceans, rivers and trees. Animals appreciate them in their water bowl or administered in diluted form with a plastic dropper.

Loreli tended to be ill at ease in thunderstorms, so I mixed her a little bottle of four or five different essences in water and labelled it 'Loreli's Thunder Medicine'. And then, if she sensed rumblings in the air, she would come to the kitchen and gaze meaningfully at the store cupboard door. After a squirt or two in her mouth, she would go peacefully to one of her little beds, instead of pacing or hiding somewhere. The essences can also be very helpful for children.

I knew practically nothing at all about flower essences, but during a three-year period in the early 90's I was suddenly and unexpectedly given the knowing and information of how and when to make them, and what they were for. I knew even less about mineral or crystal essences and learned that they were to remain in their bowl of water overnight. As the sun and the song of the birds helped the flowers release their essence, for the minerals it was more the blessing of the moon and the singing of the stars. As an example, I include a description and information of one flower essence, and a brief definition of all the others.

~ ~ ~ ~ ~

Abbreviated Definitions of the Essences

Amethyst ~ for balance, harmony, purification, and transformation. For stabilization and general support.

Blue Rock Quartz ~ supports our next quantum leap in consciousness, our intent to create and expand. Helps define purpose. Enables highest potential and clarification of Divine Will in action. Facilitates the Ascension merge. The Fly High essence.

Cherry Bark ~ for resilience and new hope. A fresh start. The 'let's begin again', the 'yes I can' essence. For overcoming hesitation, reluctance, or stressful situations. For Courage! For the dog before a visit to the Vet.

Citrine ~ resonates with the future. Empowers intent, purpose, and focus. Helps anchor the perfection of our vision, enabling a fusion of alternate realities. Assists in sustaining concentration and stamina. A catalyst.

Clematis ~ for the 'mother', to support her in the purity of her intent. For all birthing new realities or experiencing the winds of change. For those who have been too long in the birth canal! Resonates with Creation and the Life Force. Assists the flow of motion in our Ascension process. For encouragement. The essence of Emergence.

Columbine ~ stimulates revelation and divine inspiration. Aligns us with planetary unfoldment to the 5th dimensional crystalline grid of Christ Consciousness, and future Earth related truths anchored into our realm by the whales, the dolphins and Nature.

Crocosmia ~ resonates with Solar Intelligence. Fires us through the Crystal Grid into the vastness of Cosmic awareness. Helps anchor the qualities of the Higher Realms. Ascension consciousness. Power and Glory!

Danburite ~ the Ascension Essence, the Star-Light connection. For remembrance and expression of original Purity and Light Being. I AM a Sun of the Sun! Resonates with future probabilities and the Opalescent Ray of Transfiguration.

Delphinium ~ has a lightness that allows one to touch hearts with Nature, the Song of Creation, angels, devas, nature spirits and the animal kingdoms. For peace, tranquility, calmness, joy ~ and reclamation of childlike simplicity.

Dogwood Blossom for renewal of joyous and childlike enthusiasm, retrieval of sweet innocence, gentleness and Love for that inner 'Child of

Light'. Encouragement for those 'can't get going' days. Bears the frequency of Purity.

Dutch Iris ~ for unification. Symbolizes all forms of unified consciousness, from the cells in our body to the thoughts, ideas and actions of Lightworkers around the world. Signifies togetherness, Oneness, Holy Union ~ Ascension. Resonates with Christ Consciousness and the Gold and Ruby Ray of Ministering Grace.

Easter Lily ~ for joy and clarity of intent. Enthusiasm and new beginnings. Supports the transformation of our cells to a higher frequency. The essence of Purity. Celebration! Easter Lily resonates with the Resurrection Flame.

Fairy Rose ~ welcome to Earth Star baby! Nurtures all Children of Light who come to 'make new'. For the newborns, the Star Children, and those birthing new realities. A support in new surroundings and upliftment to our highest potential. The reality that all is One in consciousness ~ the reality of Ascension.

Fluorite ~ the 'letting go' essence, of the past, old habits, beliefs, and other limitations. Soothes a mind in turmoil. Encourages forgiveness. Allows serenity. May help insomnia due to an overactive mind. Bears the tone of Freedom.

Forsythia ~ promotes a richness in consciousness that opens the gateway to abundance! More laughter and friends, financial freedom, or better health. For encouragement. The essence of prosperity consciousness.

Garlic Chives offer silent encouragement in expressing our inherent strength and purity. Simplicity in action that activates a similar response from others. A very gentle essence bearing the frequency of Harmlessness.

Lapis Lazuli ~ supports all in a leader, teacher, visionary or guardianship role. For all who are physically or symbolically playing the part of father, mentor or counselor. Gives assistance in presenting new options to others.

Meidiland Rose ~ for true Love, for more Love, especially on those 'out of sync' days. Bears the frequency of Trust, the knowing that we are truly loved and supported by the Universe. The love yourself Essence ~ and reboot to Source!

Moldavite ~ for healing the rift, bridging the gap. Heals the mind of the thought or idea of the illusion of separation, between Source, others, or aspects of self. For peace and understanding. Resonates with the Tone of Tranquility.

Mountain Laurel ~ an atomic accelerator or catalyst that fires the Light codings within our molecular or bone structure, awakening us to maximum potential. Triggers the inner knowing or remembrance of transcendence ~ that consciousness continues. There is only Life. Fulfillment. Perfection! Enlightenment and Ascension!

Parsley ~ enables us to see things from a higher perspective with purer vision. Stimulates fresh insights, awareness, and wisdom. Encourages tolerance, patience and 'ah-ha's'! Promotes a quickening in consciousness and helps anchor Divine inspiration. Parsley resonates with the Green Ray of Healing and bears the quality of Illumined Truth.

Peony ~ supports one in the process of forgiveness and compassion, in surrendering, letting go of the past. Encourages Love and gentleness towards self and others. Resonates with Reverence for Life and the Spirit of Peace, allowing a free-flowing state of Grace. Helps dispel feelings of inadequacy if heartlessness to Life brings distress.

Pine Root ~ recharges, energizes and stabilizes. Helps one get out of the head and into the heart. A reminder that we are where needed. For renewal of spirit, strength, resilience and mindfulness. A grounding device for the airborne!

Rose Quartz ~ vibrates to the qualities of Love and Harmlessness. Helps bring peace and calmness to indecision or misunderstandings. Use before 'healing', sleep, meditation, or in need of nurturance and harmony. Mother Mary is affiliated with the Pink Ray with which Rose Quartz resonates, invoke assistance from her and the Angels of Love.

Sea Oats ~ for flexibility, adaptability. Helps neutralize resistance, assists in moving gracefully onward through uncertainty to expanded consciousness and the dictates of Spirit. Sea Oats bear the frequency of the oceans, whales and dolphins, the fluidity of form in motion, the resonance of change. Transformation. Enlightenment ~ Ascension!

Shasta Daisy ~ for reclamation and right use of power that was at any time lost or relinquished. Assists in severing psychic chords or attachments to any person, place, condition, or thing. Use for fear-based issues and claim your responsibilities! A powerful catalyst that resonates with the Spirit of Change, Archangel Michael and Divine Will.

Silver Maple Bark ~ offers courage in applying those inner knowings or soul promptings that must be expressed and fulfilled. Support and ally for those who feel they 'go it alone'. Resonates with the Sword of Michael, Truth & Light.

Simplicity Rose ~ for the perfectionist! For honoring self and others, just as they are. Allows that all is in Divine Order ~ in accordance with the law of free will. Bears the keynote of Acceptance, surrender to the Great I AM.

Sunchoke ~ helps anchor the reality of a higher Order of Truth and cellular remembrance of Being ~ Solar Consciousness, our soul connection with the Brotherhood of the Sun, the Order of Melchizedek. Bears the tone of Infinity, the frequency of Home, symbolic of Eternal Friendship. Resonates throughout Nature, use as a blessing for the Earth and all Life in Sacred Ceremony.

Sunflower ~ for Victory. Sovereignty. Self-mastery. For alignment with and the courage to claim our highest potential, our Birthright, Divine Inheritance and Royal Lineage. Celebrate the remembrance that I AM THAT I AM! Bears the tone of Infinity Consciousness.

Virginia Bluebells ~ encourage expression of our creative or feeling nature. Honors the purity and perfection of the Divine Mother, the Feminine Principle within all things, allowing the infinite blessings of a free-flowing state of Grace in daily life. Resonates with the frequency of Holy Spirit.

Wedding Phlox ~ for simplification of daily living. Assists in prioritizing those priorities and getting rid of the stuff, the clutter ~ in our minds also, creating space for the new. A soothing balm for bumpy transitions. A tranquilizer for Lightworkers on the go.

~ ~ ~ ~ ~

An example of the description that accompanies each essence:

Wedding Phlox *maculata* 'Miss Lingard'

A variety of the tall pink Summer Phlox. So called because it blooms in late spring, just in time for all the weddings.

On the early morning garden tour, I was quite overcome by the beauty of Miss Lingard. Earlier, smaller and daintier than her robust sisters, Miss Lingard's multiple stalks were covered in small, simple five petalled white flowers. She is so beautiful. I love her so much. What are you for? How can you help us? I all but fell to my knees in front of her little flowers, lightly tinged with palest pink. Her voice within my mind was so gentle, so loving, so pure and simple.

Yes, we are beautiful and dainty and delicate. So many of us living together in harmony and simplicity. We are to help simplify your lives. We are to help you simplify your daily living. See how we are, see how we grow together, so many of us. So close, and each in peace and beauty. Take us and call for simplification in your own lives. Allow the clutter to fall away. This applies not only to the possessions that you think you need to help you exist, it applies also to the clutter within your mind, dear ones. Allow it to go, so the beautiful thoughts of the Christed One that is your own True Self may filter through. It cannot enter, there is no place for it to be when your minds are a brim with thoughts and plans and confusion ~ on how and when and why and where you should do this or that. Allow it to go, and know that you can receive your orders, your information, your assistance at any time you need. You do not have to worry and plan.

Take us and we shall help you simplify your thoughts. Focus on beauty and peace and joy ~ and what else is there? Allow these qualities to fill your minds and make a seedbed for the one true thought, which is to honor, love and cherish your

Creator, and the beauty that He/She made for you to enjoy. And we the flowers are one expression of that beauty.

I say they are so beautiful, I do not know if I can bring myself to pick them. Gently they reply that if I do not pick them, I do not permit them to fulfill their purpose.

Wedding Phlox for simplification, eh? Who does not need the Wedding Phlox? Wedding Phlox is God's gift to the weary, a tranquilizer for Lightworkers on the go, a soothing balm for bumpy transitions. ~ The Brotherhood of Love and Light.

Summary: Wedding Phlox for simplification. Take if things appear confused or difficult and clutter seemingly rules, in mind or closet. Assists in prioritizing those priorities, letting go of the past, and allowing the truth of our Being to shine forth and focus on the beauty of Creation. Wedding Phlox allows us to take joy in that period of 'waiting', heightening the anticipation and expectancy of what is to come. It harmonizes with the Fourth Ray of Purity, Resurrection and Ascension, and helps us stay focused on what we do want.

Suggested Affirmation: "I take Wedding Phlox, and all is simplified! I AM light and clear and joyful. I AM THAT!"

Testimony: "I love the descriptions of all the essences. I still use Wedding Phlox more than anything else. I love it because it works, and I need it!" ~ Patti N, Florida

Paneurhythmy

a Celebration with Nature

*Holy Harmony in Motion.
A gift from the Celestial Realms
engaging Earth, the Cosmos ~ and you,
to prepare us for this time of Ascension.*

I include mention of Paneurhythmy because it is a regular happening in the Garden of Sananda, and because the little dogs loved it! And because it is my next book. After full investigation of any bags or baskets left lying around, the little dachshunds would join the circle, lying stretched out in the sun where each set of partners had to keep making the decision whether to step over them or deviate to one side. Eventually, there was the potluck, highlight of the little dog's day.

Paneurhythmy is a joyous celebration with all Creation. In a series of 28 easily learned movements we walk a rhythmic circle dance, balancing and honoring our expression of life in all realms of existence. The Universe and Nature support us through the music, movement and our own focused intent. Traditionally celebrated outdoors each morning between the Spring and Fall Equinox, Paneurhythmy is a joyful prayer in motion, a poetic meditation in movement. Awakening us to our highest potential, it assists on all levels of our being, promoting balance and harmony, expansion in consciousness, coordination, concentration, physical well being, a strengthening of the nervous system, beauty, grace and joy.

Paneurhythmy is suitable for all ages, and although it is designed to be 'danced' with a partner, the first ten movements are especially easy to dance alone, a joyous greeting to the new day. Each movement corresponds to a deep inner truth and reflects the awakening and unfoldment of our spiritual evolution, ideals which we broadcast to the worlds around. Paneurhythmy gives us the opportunity to show our gratitude to Mother Earth, our appreciation for the beauty and wonder of Nature, a barefoot massage in loving reverence to the land.

Based on a deep knowledge of Energy, Vibration and Consciousness, which some may know as the Seven Universal Principles of the Kybalion, and others may term Noetic Science, the music and movements of Paneurhythmy were brought forth from the celestial realms by the Bulgarian spiritual Master Peter Deunov with the conscious intent to help us through these now times of awakening and renewal ~ Ascension.

> "These movements are taken from Nature,
> from the Universe itself, thus they are in harmony
> with the Cosmic Rhythm of Life." ~ *Peter Deunov*

Peter Deunov, also known as Beinso Douno (1864-1944), was a musician and composer. His exquisite melodies and spiritual songs are played and sung by Bulgaria's leading vocalists and musicians. Frequently using Nature as his example, this Master gave discourse on every subject from family matters to stars beyond the stars, the reasons and resolution for discord and wars, and the future of humanity. He spoke of the blossoming of the human soul, and the birth of a new consciousness and culture based on Love, Wisdom and Truth ~ truths that are embedded in the movements of Paneurhythmy, first presented in Bulgaria in the 1930's

The entire Cosmos is permeated by music and movement, all Life is Paneurhythmy. Through the music we attune to Universal Rhythm and the energies of the Earth. Recharging ourselves from Nature, the circle becomes a focus for receiving and transmitting these forces, acting as a stimulus to our physical and spiritual centers.

Some have seen us, the participants, as dancing flowers! And some have seen the flowers, the nature spirits, dancing with us as we play our morning tribute to the Sun. Tidal waves of radiance flow from our hearts to the worlds around and far beyond. The Earth herself is blessed. The Master said, that whenever we dance Paneurhythmy, the Beings of Light dance with us.

> "When we dance with inner feeling and concentration,
> we harmonize with the movements of Angels ~ and all of Nature,
> who also dance Paneurhythmy." ~ *Peter Deunov*

Little is known of this Master, his music and Paneurhythmy because all spiritual concepts were banned in Bulgaria during the communist regime ~ and the Bulgarian Teachings are not easy to translate! Although spiritual contemporaries such as Einstein, Paramanhansa Yogananda, and Rudolf Steiner, all acknowledged and honored him. More recently, Wayne Dyer declared Peter Deunov his own latest and greatest spiritual teacher.

Paneurhythmy takes forty-five minutes and is based on an exchange with Nature. It may be followed by Sun Rays, an exchange with Solar energy, and Pentagrams, an exchange with universal or Cosmic Energies. Every summer, thousands gather to camp high in the Rila Mountains of Bulgaria to sing and dance Paneurhythmy, accompanied by many of Bulgaria's leading musicians and opera singers.

"When Paneurhythmy is danced in the schools,
there will be peace on Earth." ~ *Peter Deunov*

~ ~ ~ ~ ~

Abbreviated Definitions of Each Paneurhythmy Movement

"Paneurhythmy is a vast Science
which in future will be studied and applied
to implement the Great Law that promotes peace,
and harmony throughout humanity.
For this reason, I have given it to you." ~ *Peter Deunov*

1 Awakening ~ to the first day of the rest of our lives. To our highest potential and greatest good. Welcoming new opportunities for creativity, hope and joy.

2 Reconciliation ~ balancing and harmonizing all aspects of our being through heart resonance ~ our relationship with each other, with Nature, the Universe, and our Self, in gentleness and love.

3 Giving ~ and receiving, the inbreath and the outbreath. Giving our gratitude and appreciation for the beauty and joy of Nature. Offering our compassion, encouragement, divine inspiration and hope in Service to the One.

4 Ascending ~ reaching upward with alternate hands to touch the Sun, the One, the eternal Source of all our joy and wonder. Ever seeking the divine connection. Renewal. Evolution on the go!

5 Elevating ~ reaching upward with both hands to claim this Goodness, becoming a holy conduit for the Cosmic Waves of Power and Light in action, the empowerment that sustains us in our Ascension, our return to Light.

6 Opening ~ to the worlds around, to incoming possibilities and opportunities ~ to the future. Connecting to the greater circle or wheel of Life that surrounds us. Expanding our realm of conscious awareness.

7 Liberation ~ joyfully letting go of the past, our limitations, attachments, outdated beliefs, habits, behaviors and problems that are not ours to solve. Parting with all that does not resonate with our Ascension process!

8 Clapping ~ rejoicing at our victory over the past! Celebrating our freedom, asserting our new way of living and being ~ in gladness and Light. Claiming our Power and Sovereignty in joy.

9 Purifying ~ our thoughts, our ideals, and expanded consciousness. Purifying with the Holy Breath our new awareness, the patterns of perfection established in the previous movements.

10 Flying ~ in remembrance of our spiritual freedom ~ together as One! With a rhythmic undulating flying motion ~ I AM, we are the next life-wave coming!

11 Evera ~ 'born of the Sun'. Blending the universal forces of Spirit with Nature. Flowing with the music, becoming one with The Way ~ The Way of Love, Wisdom and Truth.

12 Jumping ~ with a joyful jump and clap of our hands we celebrate our joy. Reaching for the Sun ~ bringing Sound to Life. Symbolically uniting Heaven and Earth.

13 Weaving ~ consciously moving forward together, weaving the new 5th dimensional crystalline solar light frequencies into the cellular structure of ourselves, our cells, and the Earth. Each step forming a new pattern of existence ~ of highest ideals and principles.

14 Think ~ think right! Invoking, applying and expanding Divine Thought in and through our daily lives. Including right action or conduct, reverential and compassionate mindfulness of all things, especially in Nature.

15 Aum ~ with alternating hands upstretched towards the sun we tone the sacred sound, offering ourselves as a divine channel between spirit and matter, Mother Earth and Father Sky. Aum is considered the most sacred of all the Paneurhythmy movements.

16 The Rising Sun ~ movements that symbolize the birth of a new Dawn. Each day we are born again, we are all brand new, replenishing and embodying the solar energies of the rising sun ~ an exchange between ourselves and Source, ourselves and Nature.

17 Square ~ gathering the qualities of the four directions. Embodying and broadcasting the eternal principles of Love, Wisdom, Truth & Justice (or Goodness). Honoring the four great Archangels, Uriel, Raphael, Michael and Gabriel who stand watch at the cardinal points.

18 Beauty ~ gently we process these powerful qualities. Beauty transforms in a creative way and as we honor the beauty and purity that is all around, we fill with more Love and become lighter on all levels of our being.

19 Agility ~ continuing integration with the frequency of the Square, we practice flexibility, physically, and in our mind, our thoughts, choices, feelings and emotions ~ becoming ever more patient and accepting.

20 Overcoming ~ free of the past, we step forth in power, with joy and enthusiasm. Confident and lively, with triumph and gladness we direct our energies, our thoughts and actions forward and up, empowering our self and all. Celebrating our victory, intending highest outcome ~ our Ascension.

21 Joy of the Earth ~ gently and joyfully, we caress and flow divine blessings of love and gratitude into the Earth and all therein ~ the nature spirits, the insects, the inner earth beings. Ever a conduit, giving and receiving, exchanging energies between Earth and Sun.

22 Acquaintance ~ for the first time we make physical contact, taking our partners hands, and with soft eye contact we acknowledge this treasured connection and shared delight. Honoring the Love, Wisdom and Truth within each. Honoring 'another-myself'.

23 Beautiful Day ~ with our partner, we acknowledge this beautiful new day we have created together. Strengthened and empowered, together as One. Our gratitude for each other and All That Is fosters peace, serenity, balance and harmony for all.

24 How Happy We Are ~ taking our partners hand in acknowledgement that we cannot sustain our enthusiasm and fulfil our purpose and reason for being on our own ~ it is a co-creative endeavor. Joyful and active, radiating happiness and gratitude to all, we dance our joy into being.

25 Step by Step ~ the way of the disciple. Time to center, consider and think, to harmonize, balance and stabilize all the previous joy and expansion. Step by step, thus do we grow, thus do we evolve ~ one step at a time.

26 Early in the Morning ~ the wrap up exercise! Bringing everything together, energizing, balancing, and projecting all we have activated into this present moment. Broadcasting the new light patternings of sacred geometries, the finer frequencies of the ideals and realities we have been embodying, into the worlds around.

27 Breathing ~ in rhythm with the music, which may be only a single violin note, we tone our way up and down the spectrum of rainbow lights, merging with our surroundings, and know Peace on Earth. The toning should be gently audible. Our breath is our connection to Source.

28 Blessing ~ "May the Peace of God abide, and the Pure Joy of God arise in our hearts forever." Raised hand in silent greeting to All Creation.

> "Nothing else is demanded of you
> but to be in harmony with the entire Universe."
> ~ *Peter Deunov (Beinsa Douno)*

About the Author

Born and raised in England, June Sananjaleen Hughes is an author and gardener who has offered workshops and playdays in Energy Healing, Interspecies Communication, Make Your Own Flower Essence, and the joyful celestial dance of Paneurhythmy.

She has been a professional horsewoman, world traveler, photographer, and Quantum Touch Instructor. She has four books on Amazon and 32 flower and mineral remedies, the Sananda Ascension Essences from her magical garden in Virginia ~ home of the ten highly evolved little longhaired Dachshunds. Now she enjoys pet-sitting the neighbors' little dogs.

June has taught riding in the Holy Land, and to Aborigine children in Australia. She has also picked beans in Tasmania, been a waitress in the Yukon, and was a jillaroo (female cowboy) on sheep and cattle stations in the outback ~ of Australia!

June Sananjaleen Hughes

sananda444@gmail.com
www.gardenofsananda.com

www.ingramcontent.com/pod-product-compliance
Lightning Source LLC
LaVergne TN
LVHW051830080426
835512LV00018B/2800